ESSENTIALS OF AI
and
SOFT COMPUTING

ANUJ SHARMA, Ph.D
Associate Professor
Department of Computer Science and Applications
Panjab University, Chandigarh

PHI Learning Private Limited
Delhi-110092
2025

*In fond memory of **Shri Asoke K. Ghosh** (October 1942 – February 2024), Founder Chairman and Managing Director of PHI Learning, whose vision endlessly inspires.*

The Legacy Continues....

Published by Pushpita Ghosh, PHI Learning Private Limited, Rimjhim House, 111, Patparganj Industrial Estate, Delhi-110092 and Gopsons Printers Pvt. Ltd., A-14, Sector-60, Noida, Gautambudh Nagar, Noida, Uttar Pradesh-201301.

₹425.00

ESSENTIALS OF AI AND SOFT COMPUTING
Anuj Sharma

ISBN-978-93-5443-990-2 (Print Book)
ISBN-978-93-5443-989-6 (e-Book)

The export rights of the book are vested solely with the publisher.

To

My Readers

May this book inspire and empower you to reach your full potential

Contents

Preface

Artificial intelligence, once confined to the realms of science fiction, has emerged as one of the most transformative technologies of our time. As we stand on the threshold of a new era, where machines can learn, reason and interact with us in increasingly sophisticated ways, it becomes imperative to understand both the promises and perils that accompany this advancement. In this book, I aim to demystify the complex landscape of artificial intelligence and soft computing, offering readers a comprehensive yet accessible guide to its principles, applications and implications. Drawing upon my years of research and teaching experience in the field, I hope to provide a roadmap for navigating through the intricacies of artificial intelligence and soft computing, from its theoretical underpinnings to its real-world implementations.

The book is more than just a technical text or manual; it is a call to action. As artificial intelligence continues to permeate every aspect of our lives, from healthcare and finance to transportation and entertainment, we are also grappled with profound questions about the ethics, accountability and the very nature of intelligence itself. Through thoughtful reflection and informed discourse, we can shape a future where artificial intelligence serves as a force for good, enriching our lives and empowering us to tackle humanity's most pressing challenges.

In an ever-evolving landscape of computational methodologies, soft computing stands out as a beacon of flexibility and adaptability. Rooted in the principles of tolerance for imprecision, uncertainty and partial truth, soft computing offers a paradigm that complements traditional computing techniques, enabling us to tackle complex real-world problems with a greater degree of nuance and sophistication. This book is a culmination of my fascination with soft computing and its myriad applications across a diverse array of disciplines. From artificial intelligence and machine learning to optimization and control systems, soft computing techniques have proven to be invaluable tools for modeling and solving problems that defy precise mathematical formulation. My journey into the realm of soft computing has been both enlightening and humbling. Through years of research and experimentation, I have come to appreciate the subtle interplay between fuzzy logic, neural networks, evolutionary algorithms and other soft computing methodologies. But more importantly, I have witnessed the transformative impact that these approaches can have on our ability to address real-world challenges in the fields as diverse as engineering, healthcare, finance and beyond.

This book is intended to serve as a comprehensive guide to the theory, algorithms and applications of soft computing. Whether you are a student or seasoned practitioner seeking to expand your toolkit or a curious newcomer eager to explore the frontiers of artificial intelligence and computational intelligence, I hope that you will find this book to be a valuable resource. As we embark on this intellectual odyssey together, I invite you to approach the subject of artificial intelligence with an open mind and a sense of wonder. For in the boundless expanse of human ingenuity, the possibilities are limited only by our imagination.

Contents and Organization

The book includes twelve chapters, and each chapter provides conceptual questions at the end. The needful bibliography has been given at the end of the book.

- Chapter 1 includes introduction, history and applications to artificial intelligence.
- Chapter 2 discusses Artificial intelligence-based state-space representation, including details of common problems. Further, problem characteristics are discussed.
- Chapter 3 is about search techniques where respective algorithms are discussed in detail.
- Chapter 4 is about explaining knowledge representation including different types to represent knowledge. Further, resolution principle has been explained with examples.
- Chapter 5 includes expert system characteristics and its related examples. Further, natural language processing stages have been explained in detail.
- Chapter 6 introduces soft computing and its various popular techniques. Further, applications of soft computing are also discussed.
- Chapter 7 is about artificial neural networks where detailed architecture of artificial neural networks has been discussed including its major components. Further, we have explained supervised and unsupervised learning and the self-organizing map has been discussed as a part of unsupervised method.
- Chapter 8 explains the the popular classification techniques alongwith their algorithms and software code.

- Chapter 9 is about clustering techniques that includes their respective algorithms and its details.
- Chapter 10 explains common dimension reduction techniques and its use in applications.
- Chapter 11 introduces fuzzy logic systems with necessary explanation of fuzzy logic basics and sequential flow of fuzzy logic components. Further, fuzzy logic has been discussed with the help of examples for clear understanding.
- Chapter 12 throws light on concepts of genetic algorithms which include components of genetic algorithms and their necessary details. This chapter includes example based study and software code to explain the concept.
- Bibliography includes references that could further help readers to explore selective topics discussed in the book.

I invite readers to share constructive feedback and suggestions for further improvement of this text.

Anuj Sharma

Acknowledgements

I would like to extend my heartfelt thanks to all those who have supported and contributed to the creation of this book. First and foremost, I am deeply grateful to parents and teachers for their invaluable blessings and encouragement in my career. A special thanks to Professor Kalpana Dahiya for providing research assistance, offering critical reviews, and valuable insight in writing process. I am also thankful to my colleagues in Panjab University, Chandigarh, especially Department of Computer Science and Applications, for their kind cooperation, support and access to resources. I am deeply thankful to all the students I have had the privilege of teaching. These student's enthusiasm, curiosity, and feedback have greatly helped in improving this book. Each one of my students has made a meaningful contribution. I am thankful to the PHI publisher's staff for all their help during the writing of this book.

To my family and friends, thank you for your unwavering patience and understanding during the many hours I spent working on this book. Your encouragement and love have been a constant source of motivation. I would like to acknowledge Alisha and Kalpana, whose support has made the completion of this book possible.

Thank you all for your invaluable contributions.

Anuj Sharma

CHAPTER 1

Introduction

1.1 ARTIFICIAL INTELLIGENCE

Artificial Intelligence (AI) is a branch of computer science that aims to create machines or systems that can perform tasks that would typically require human intelligence. The two words "artificial" and "intelligence" mean 'man made' and 'potential to solve problems' as humans do. We can view AI from the perspective of a variety of tasks like learning, reasoning, problem-solving, perception and language understanding. AI systems are designed to mimic human cognitive functions and can be used in a wide range of applications, from self-driving cars and virtual assistants to medical diagnosis and game playing.

There are several approaches to AI, including *symbolic AI*, which involves the use of logical symbols to represent knowledge and reasoning processes, and *machine learning*, which uses algorithms to learn patterns and make predictions from data. Deep learning, a subset of machine learning, has been particularly successful in recent years, achieving breakthroughs in areas like image recognition and natural language processing. Today, AI has revolutionised our lives, as it is being used for real-life applications. Recently, Large Language Models (LLM) have attracted users from all domains and the magic of AI is clearly visible.

1.1.1 AI Tasks

The common tasks performed by AI are formal, mundane and expert in nature. The early work in AI focused on formal tasks, such as game playing and theorem proving. The *formal tasks* relate to problems where human intelligence is visible. The *mundane tasks* are perception based, Natural Language Processing (NLP) and robotic control etc. Perception problems mainly include computer vision problems, speech and voice recognition etc. Today, NLP problems are associated with LLM. Humans have the ability to solve mundane tasks by birth with surrounding experiences and machines need to train with domain associated data. The *expert tasks* are commonly associated with medical diagnosis, financial analysis, weather forecasting, engineering designing etc. It has been observed that these three AI tasks as formal, mundane and expert-based applications include properties from one or more tasks.

1.1.2 AI Techniques

Artificial intelligence-based solutions can be applied to a broad spectrum of tasks. It has been observed that AI techniques can be employed for almost all conceivable human activities. However, the challenge remains in addressing the complexities inherent in various tasks. Knowledge is the main requisite for all forms of intelligence, and it can be vast, variable and dependent on data structures. AI leverages this knowledge to address challenges and corrects knowledge as data changes, capturing generalizations and grouping common elements together. This further helps to overcome memory issues in systems. The errors could be rectified for knowledge using AI. The three components of AI techniques are search, use of knowledge and abstraction. The search is applicable to many problems to be solved where no direct solutions are possible. Also, an easy framework provides solutions to solve other problems where direct solutions are not possible. The use of knowledge is systematic, as discussed above. Abstraction provides a way to separate important features and variations from many unrelated aspects of the problem domain.

In today's AI developments, these techniques can vary widely depending on the specific task or problem being addressed. Some common AI techniques include machine learning, deep learning, natural language processing, computer vision, robotics, and more. Each AI technique is designed to solve a particular set of problems or to perform specific tasks. For example, machine learning techniques are used to develop algorithms that can learn from and make predictions based on data, whereas natural language processing techniques are used to enable computers to understand and generate human language. AI techniques are constantly evolving as researchers and developers seek more efficient and effective ways to build intelligent systems. As a result, new techniques are regularly being developed and existing techniques are being refined and improved. Some of the popular AI techniques are machine learning, deep learning, NLP, computer vision, robotics, expert systems, fuzzy logics and genetic algorithms etc. These are just a few of the many techniques used in AI. As the field continues to evolve, new techniques and approaches are constantly being developed to tackle increasingly complex problems.

1.1.3 Classification of AI

AI is classified as weak, strong and evolutionary.

- **Weak or Narrow AI** includes study and design of machines that perform intelligent tasks. The way tasks are performed is not a concern of weak AI, but its performance and efficiency are the main concern. It is focused on addressing a particular problem and does not possess general intelligence or the ability to understand and learn any task like a human. Examples of narrow AI include virtual assistants, recommendation systems, and autonomous vehicles.

- **Strong AI** focuses on the design of machines that simulate the human mind to perform intelligent tasks. This mainly includes ideas from surroundings, solvable in a way the human mind operates. The strong AI systems have the ability to understand, learn, and apply knowledge across a wide range of tasks, similar to human intelligence. These systems would be capable of reasoning, problem-solving, and learning new tasks without being explicitly programmed for them. Strong AI is still largely theoretical and complicated in nature that makes it complex to achieve goals successfully.
- **Evolutionary AI** simulates simple creatures, and attempts to evolve and have higher level emergent behavior. The evolutionary AI competes with human intelligence in various ways. This type of intelligence is considered to be a potential future development, and its implications and consequences are subjects of significant environmental processes and speculation within the AI research outcomes.

1.2 HISTORY AND DEVELOPMENT OF AI

The history and development of AI can be traced back to ancient times, with early ideas and concepts emerging in Greek mythology and ancient civilizations. However, the modern field of AI began to take shape in the mid-20th century. The Turing machine invented by Alan Turing in 1936 proved to be a milestone in the computing world, which he further demonstrated with the Turing test in 1950. The AI as a field, brought together researchers John McCarthy, Marvin Minsky, Nathaniel Rochester and Claude Shannon to explore the possibility of creating machines that could simulate human intelligence in 1956. In the 1950s and 1960s, researchers developed some of the first AI programs, such as the Logic Theorist and the General Problem Solver. These programs were capable of solving mathematical problems and logic puzzles. During 1970-80, AI research focused on symbolic AI, which used logic and symbols to represent knowledge and reasoning. Expert systems, which mimicked the decision-making processes of human experts in specific domains, became popular. Many new algorithms were introduced, mainly related to neural networks from 1980 to 2000. Also, advancements in robotics were witnessed during these years.

After 2000, many machine learning-based algorithms were introduced and the field of deep learning helped to popularise AI. The advancements in AI today are based on collective efforts of research in the past and innovation in hardware that supported the applications to achieve goals. Notably applications such as image recognition, Natural Language Processing, and autonomous vehicles have seen significant advancements. Today, AI technologies are integrated into many aspects of daily life, from virtual assistants and recommendation systems to healthcare and finance. However, AI also raises ethical, social, and economic challenges, such as job displacement, bias in algorithms, and privacy concerns. Throughout its history, AI has been a field of both great promise and significant challenges. As researchers continue to push the boundaries of what is possible, the future of AI holds the potential for profound impacts on society and technology.

1.2.1 Turing Test

The Turing Test is a concept introduced by Alan Turing in 1950. The test is designed to assess a machine's ability to exhibit intelligent behavior indistinguishable from that of a human. The Turing test includes the following steps:

- **Setup:** The test involves a human evaluator who interacts with both a human and a machine through a voice or text-based interface, such as a chat program. The evaluator is unaware of which interlocutor is human and which is a machine.
- **Objective:** The objective of the test is for the machine to generate responses that are indistinguishable from human responses, so that the evaluator cannot reliably determine which is which.
- **Criteria:** Turing proposed that if the machine is able to fool the evaluator into believing it is human more number of times during a series of defined time slabs for an AI program, then the machine can be said to possess human-level intelligence.

The Turing Test has been a foundational concept in the field of artificial intelligence and has sparked significant debate about the nature of intelligence and the potential for machines to exhibit human-like capabilities. While no machine has yet passed a strict interpretation of the Turing Test, it remains a benchmark for assessing progress in AI research.

1.3 APPLICATIONS OF AI

AI has a wide range of applications across various industries and fields. Some of the key applications include:

- **Healthcare:** AI is used for medical image analysis, personalized treatment plans, drug discovery, and patient management.
- **Finance:** AI is used for fraud detection, algorithmic trading, risk assessment, and customer service.
- **Autonomous Vehicles:** AI is used for object detection, path planning, and decision-making in self-driving cars.

- **Retail:** AI is used for demand forecasting, personalized recommendations, inventory management, and customer service.
- **Manufacturing:** AI is used for predictive maintenance, quality control, supply chain optimization, and robotics.
- **Natural Language Processing (NLP):** AI is used for language translation, sentiment analysis, chatbots, and speech recognition.
- **Gaming:** AI is used for creating realistic game environments, opponent modeling, and game strategy optimization.
- **Smart Homes:** AI is used for home automation, energy management, and security systems.
- **Education:** AI is used for personalized learning, intelligent tutoring systems, and educational content creation.
- **Marketing:** AI is used for targeted advertising, customer segmentation, and campaign optimization.

In addition to the above mentioned applications of AI, it continues to grow and evolve rapidly.

EXERCISES

1.1 What is Artificial Intelligence? How is Artificial Intelligence related to human intelligence?

1.2 What are Artificial Intelligence tasks? Discuss each task with suitable examples.

1.3 How mundane and formal tasks are different from each other in Artificial Intelligence? Is there any possibility of an example that is part of both tasks as mundane and formal?

1.4 What are AI techniques? Discuss using examples.

1.5 What are AI classification types? List each type with suitable examples.

1.6 Differentiate between weak and strong AI.

1.7 How is evolutionary AI different from strong and weak AI? Give examples of evolutionary AI.

1.8 What is the Turing test? How is it performed? Draw a diagram to depict the Turing test for an example.

1.9 Discuss history and development of AI step-by-step. How's John McCarthy related to AI development?

1.10 List AI applications in today's era. What potential AI applications could be developed in the near future?

CHAPTER 2

State-Space Representation

2.1 WHAT IS STATE-SPACE REPRESENTATION?

A state-space representation is a way to model the possible states of a problem and the transitions between these states. A state space is the set of all states reachable from the initial state. It is commonly used in AI for search algorithms, planning, and decision-making processes. In a state-space representation for AI:

- Each state represents a configuration or situation of the problem;
- The transitions between states are determined by actions or operators;
- The goal is to find a sequence of actions that lead from the initial state to a goal state.
- A state space forms a graph in which the nodes are states and the arcs between nodes are actions. In state space, a path is a sequence of states connected by a sequence of actions. The solution of a problem is part of the graph formed by the state space.

For example, in a simple robotic navigation problem, the states could represent different positions of the robot on a grid, and the actions could be its movements in different directions. The state-space representation helps the AI algorithm explore the possible actions and make decisions to reach the goal state.

State-space representation is fundamental in AI because it allows complex problems to be represented and solved in a structured and efficient manner. The selected examples to implement state-space representation are discussed below:

2.1.1 Water-Jug Problem

The water-jug problem is a classic problem in artificial intelligence that involves using two jugs to measure a specific amount of water. The problem is stated as follows:

You are given two jugs, a 4-gallon jug and a 3-gallon jug, and a water faucet. The jugs do not have markings to indicate partial volumes. You are tasked with measuring out exactly 2 gallons of water using these jugs. To represent this problem in state-space form, we define the following components:

- **State:** A state in this problem can be represented by the current amounts of water in the 4-gallon jug and the 3-gallon jug. For example, if the 4-gallon jug is full and the 3-gallon jug is empty, the state can be represented as $(4,0)$.
- **Initial State:** The initial state is the starting configuration of the jugs, which is usually $(0,0)$, indicating both jugs are initially empty.
- **Goal State:** The goal state is the state where we have exactly 2 gallons of water in one of the jugs. In this case, the goal state could be $(2,x)$ or $(x,2)$, where x is any value between 0 and 4.
- **Actions:** The actions in this problem are the operations we can perform to change the state of the jugs. The actions can be filling a jug, emptying a jug, or pouring water from one jug to another until the target jug is full or the source jug is empty.
- **Transition Model:** The transition model describes how the actions change the state of the jugs. For example, if we pour water from jug A to jug B, the new state will be (A′ B′), where A′ and B′ are the new amounts of water in the jugs after pouring.

Using this representation, we can apply a suitable algorithm to find a sequence of actions that lead from the initial state to the goal state, thus solving the water jug problem.

2.1.2 8-Puzzle Problem

The 8-puzzle problem is typically represented using a state-space representation in AI. The 8-puzzle problem can be represented as:

- **State:** A state in the 8-puzzle problem is represented by the arrangement of the 8 tiles on the 3×3 board, along with the position of the empty space. Each tile can be represented by a number from 1 to 8, and the empty space can be represented by 0. The initial and goal states are depicted in Figure 2.1.

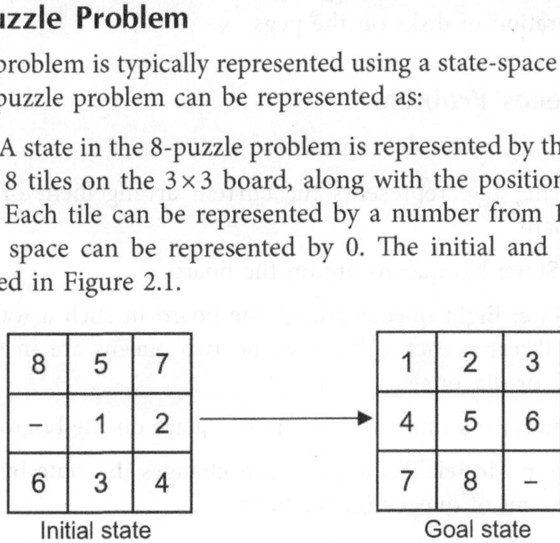

Figure 2.1 Initial and goal states of 8-Puzzle game.

- **Initial State:** The initial state is the starting configuration of the puzzle. It can be any valid arrangement of the tiles.
- **Goal State:** The goal state is the desired configuration of the puzzle, as in the Figure 2.1, increasing order of tile's numbers, row-wise.
- **Actions:** The actions in this problem are the moves that can be made to change the state of the puzzle. The possible moves are to slide a tile adjacent to the empty space into the empty space.
- **Transition Model:** The transition model describes how the actions change the state of the puzzle.

Using this representation, various search algorithms can be applied to find a sequence of moves that lead from the initial state to the goal state, solving the 8-puzzle problem.

2.1.3 Tower of Hanoi Problem

The Tower of Hanoi problem is common in recursive programming. It can be represented as:

- **State:** The state consists of the configuration of disks on three pegs.
- **Initial State:** All disks are on the first peg, arranged from largest (bottom) to smallest (top).
- **Goal State:** All disks are on the third peg, in the same order as the initial state.
- **Actions:** Move the top disk from one peg to another. A disk can only be placed on top of a larger disk or an empty peg.
- **Transition Model:** Moving a disk changes the state by updating the configuration of disks on the pegs.

2.1.4 8-queens Problem

The 8-queens problem can be represented as:

- **State:** The state represents the current arrangement of queens on a chessboard.
- **Initial State:** No queens are on the board.
- **Goal State:** Eight queens are on the board in such a way that no two queens threaten each other (i.e., no two queens are in the same row, column, or diagonal).
- **Actions:** Place a queen in an empty square on the board.
- **Transition Model:** Placing a queen changes the state by updating the arrangement of queens on the board.

2.2 PRODUCTION SYSTEM

A production system is a fundamental concept used to represent knowledge-based systems. It consists of a set of rules or production rules, along with mechanisms for applying these rules to a given state or set of conditions. Production systems are widely used in areas such as expert systems, rule-based reasoning, and problem-solving tasks.

The production system typically works as:

- **Knowledge Base:** The knowledge base contains a set of rules or production rules. These rules encode knowledge about the domain, problem-solving strategies, or decision-making criteria. Each rule typically has two parts: a condition (also known as the "antecedent" or "if" part) and an action (also known as the "consequent" or "then" part).
- **Inference Engine:** The inference engine is responsible for applying the rules in the knowledge base to the current state of the system. It matches the conditions of the rules against the current state to determine which rules are applicable.
- **Rule Execution:** When the conditions of a rule match the contents of the working memory, the corresponding action is executed. This may involve modifying the working memory (adding, deleting, or updating facts) or performing some other computational task.
- **Control Strategy:** The control strategy determines the order in which rules are selected and applied. Different strategies, such as depth-first, breadth-first, or best-first, can be used to prioritise rule execution based on factors such as relevance, efficiency, or specific problem-solving objectives.

Production systems provide an excellent tool for structuring AI programs. Production systems are module based and individual rules can be added, removed or modified independently. The production rules are expressed in a natural form, so the statements contained in the knowledge base should be easily understandable. Production systems are particularly suited for tasks that involve symbolic reasoning, pattern matching, and rule-based decision-making. They are often used in expert systems, where domain-specific knowledge can be represented as a set of rules and applied to solve problems or provide advice in a particular field. While production systems offer flexibility and transparency in representing knowledge and reasoning processes, they may face challenges in handling uncertainty, complex interactions, and large-scale knowledge bases. In such cases, hybrid approaches combining production systems with other AI techniques, such as probabilistic reasoning or machine learning, may be employed to address these challenges and improve system performance.

Main characteristics of the production system are monotonicity, non-monotonicity, commutativity, and partial commutativity. These are discussed below:

- **Monotonicity** in a production system implies that the addition of more knowledge or information never invalidates or reverses previous conclusions. In other words, as more evidence or data is gathered, the system's beliefs may stay the same or become more certain, but they never change to become less certain.

  Example: In a diagnostic system, if additional symptoms are observed, the system should either maintain its diagnosis or refine it further but never retract it based solely on new information.

- **Non-monotonicity** refers to the ability of a system to revise previously reached conclusions in light of new evidence or information, even if that new evidence doesn't directly contradict the existing conclusions.

  Example: In a default reasoning system, a conclusion may be reached based on incomplete or default information. However, if more specific evidence becomes available, the system may revise its conclusion.

- **Commutativity** refers to the property where the order of operations does not affect the final result. In the context of production systems, it means that the order of applying rules or actions does not affect the system's output.

  Example: In a rule-based system for scheduling tasks, the order in which tasks are scheduled should not affect the overall schedule's outcome if the tasks are independent of each other.

- **Partial Commutativity** means that some operations or rules in the system commute while others may not. In other words, certain actions or rules can be reordered without affecting the final outcome, but not all actions or rules exhibit this property.

  Example: In a multi-agent system, where agents interact to achieve a common goal, certain actions of one agent may be commutative with the action of another agent. However, not all actions have this property.

Incorporating these characteristics into an AI production system can significantly impact its behavior and applicability in various domains. Monotonicity and non-monotonicity influence the system's ability to reason under uncertainty and adapt to changing circumstances, while commutativity and partial commutativity can affect the system's efficiency and robustness in handling concurrent or distributed operations. Understanding and appropriately leveraging these characteristics are essential for designing effective and reliable AI systems.

2.3 PROBLEM CHARACTERISTICS

In artificial intelligence (AI), problem characteristics play a crucial role in determining the suitability of different AI techniques and algorithms for solving specific problems. Some of the key problem characteristics commonly considered in AI are as follows:

- **Complexity:** The complexity of a problem refers to the number of variables, dependencies, and interactions involved. Problems may range from simple, well-defined tasks to highly complex, ambiguous situations. AI techniques such as search algorithms, constraint satisfaction, and optimization methods are used to tackle problems of varying complexity.
- **Uncertainty:** Many real-world problems involve uncertainty due to incomplete or noisy data, ambiguous input, or unpredictable environments. Probabilistic reasoning, Bayesian networks, and fuzzy logic are AI techniques that can handle uncertainty and make decisions under incomplete information.
- **Dynamicity:** Some problems are dynamic, meaning they evolve over time or involve changing conditions. Dynamic problems require AI systems to adapt and react to new information or events. Techniques such as reinforcement learning and online learning are suitable for addressing dynamic problems.
- **Scalability:** Scalability refers to the ability of an AI system to handle increasing problem sizes efficiently. Problems may grow in size in terms of input data, complexity, or computational requirements. Scalable AI techniques, such as parallel computing, distributed algorithms, and approximation methods, are essential for addressing large-scale problems.
- **Interactivity:** Interactive problems involve interactions between the AI system and human users or other systems. These problems often require real-time responses and feedback mechanisms. AI techniques such as natural language processing, dialogue systems, and interactive learning are used to address interactive problems.
- **Multi-agent:** Some problems involve multiple agents or entities with conflicting objectives or cooperative behavior. Multi-agent systems require AI techniques that can model interactions, negotiate agreements, and coordinate actions among different agents. Game theory, multi-agent reinforcement learning, and distributed optimization are used to address multi-agent problems.
- **Non-determinism:** Non-deterministic problems exhibit randomness or unpredictability in their outcomes. These problems may arise in stochastic environments or systems with inherent randomness. AI techniques such as Monte Carlo methods, simulated annealing, and evolutionary algorithms are used to address non-deterministic problems.

- **Constraint Satisfaction:** Some problems involve satisfying a set of constraints or conditions while optimizing certain objectives. Constraint satisfaction problems require AI techniques that can efficiently explore solution spaces and satisfy all constraints. Constraint programming, local search, and constraint propagation are used to address constraint satisfaction problems.

Understanding the characteristics of a problem is essential for selecting the most appropriate AI techniques and algorithms to solve it effectively. Different AI approaches excel in addressing specific types of problems, and considering characteristics of the problem helps in identifying the best-suited approach for a given problem domain.

EXERCISES

2.1 What is state-space representation? How does it help in solving a problem? Give a few examples of state-space search.

2.2 Solve water-jug problem, with two jugs of capacity 4 liters and 3 liters, respectively. The jugs do not have any marker and water supply is unlimited. Discuss all rules and steps that result in 2 liters of water in any jug.

2.3 Discuss the 8-queen problem as a state-space search example.

2.4 Discuss the tic-tac-toe problem as a state-space search example.

2.5 Discuss the 8-Puzzle problem as a state-space search example.

2.6 Discuss the tower of hanoi problem as a state-space search example.

2.7 What are problem characteristics? Why these are important in solving AI problem?

2.8 Write short note on problem characteristics.

2.9 Discuss in detail for production system.

2.10 List important components of production system.

2.11 Discuss production system characteristics.

CHAPTER 3

Search Techniques

3.1 SEARCH TECHNIQUES AND ITS TYPES

In artificial intelligence, search algorithms can be categorized into two main types based on the amount of domain knowledge they use: uninformed search and informed search. These are explained as:

- **Uninformed Search Algorithms**, also known as blind search algorithms, do not have any additional domain-specific knowledge about the problem beyond the information provided in the problem definition. These algorithms explore the search space systematically without considering the specific characteristics of the problem or the goal state. Examples of uninformed search algorithms include Depth-First Search (DFS) and Breadth-First Search (BFS).
- **Informed Search Algorithms**, also known as heuristic search algorithms, leverage domain-specific knowledge or heuristics to guide the search process more effectively towards the goal state. These algorithms use additional information, typically in the form of heuristic functions, to estimate the desirability of different search paths. Informed search algorithms generally make more informed decisions about which paths to explore, potentially leading to more efficient and effective search. Examples of informed search algorithms include generate and test, hill climbing, best first search, A* and AO* Search.

The *uninformed* and *informed* searches are distinguished on the following basis:

- **Knowledge Base:** Uninformed search algorithms rely solely on the structure of the search space and do not use any additional domain-specific knowledge.
  Informed search algorithms leverage domain-specific knowledge or heuristics to guide the search process more effectively.

- **Efficiency:** Uninformed search algorithms may explore a large portion of the search space, potentially leading to inefficiency, especially in large or complex problem domains.
  Informed search algorithms tend to be more efficient as they focus on more promising paths and avoid exploring unpromising ones.
- **Completeness and Optimality:** Uninformed search algorithms such as BFS are generally complete and optimal, meaning they are guaranteed to find a solution if one exists and they find the shortest solution path. Informed search algorithms may sacrifice completeness or optimality for efficiency, depending on the quality of the heuristic function used.
- **Domain Specific Issues:** Uninformed search algorithms can be applied to a wide range of problems where little or no domain-specific knowledge is available.
  Informed search algorithms are particularly effective in domains where heuristic information can be readily defined and used to guide the search process.

3.2 BREADTH-FIRST SEARCH

Breadth-First Search (BFS) is an algorithm used to traverse or search tree or graph data structures. It starts at a specified node (often referred to as the "root" node) and explores all the neighbor nodes at the present depth level before moving on to the nodes at the next depth level. The key characteristic of BFS is that it systematically explores the search space level by level, visiting all the nodes at a given depth before moving on to nodes at the next depth level. This approach ensures that nodes are visited in increasing order of their distance from the starting node. BFS is commonly used for: finding the shortest path from a starting node to a goal node in an unweighted graph or tree, traversing or searching tree or graph data structures and detecting cycles in a graph.

The algorithm uses a data structure called a queue to keep track of nodes to be visited. It follows the First-In-First-Out (FIFO) principle, meaning that nodes are visited in the order they were added to the queue. Breadth-First Search algorithm works as discussed in Algorithm 1.

Algorithm 1 Breadth-First Search

Start with the root node and enqueue it into the queue.

While *the queue is not empty* **do**

- Dequeue a node from the front of the queue.
- Process the dequeued node (e.g., print its value or perform some operation).
- Enqueue all non visited neighbor nodes of the dequeued node into the queue.

end

By systematically exploring the search space level by level, BFS guarantees that it will find the shortest path from the starting node to any other reachable node in an unweighted graph or tree.

3.3 DEPTH-FIRST SEARCH

Depth-First Search (DFS) is an algorithm used for traversing or searching tree or graph data structures. Unlike Breadth-First Search (BFS), which explores all the neighbor nodes at the present depth level before moving on to the nodes at the next depth level, DFS explores as far as possible along each branch before backtracking. The key characteristic of DFS is that it systematically explores the search space by traversing one branch of the search tree as deeply as possible before backtracking. This approach can be visualized as "going deep" into the search space before "backtracking" and exploring other branches. DFS is commonly used for: traversing or searching tree or graph data structures, finding paths; cycles, or connected components in a graph, topological sorting of directed acyclic graphs. The algorithm typically uses a stack data structure to keep track of nodes to be visited. It follows the Last-In-First-Out (LIFO) principle, meaning that nodes are visited in the reverse order of their exploration. Depth-First Search algorithm has been explained in Algorithm 2.

Algorithm 2 Depth-First Search

Start with the root node and push it onto the stack.
While *the stack is not empty* **do**

- ♦ Pop a node from the top of the stack.
- ♦ Process the popped node (e.g., print its value or perform some operation).
- ♦ Push all unvisited neighbor nodes of the popped node onto the stack.

end

By systematically exploring one branch of the search tree as deeply as possible before backtracking, DFS can be more memory-efficient than BFS for searching large or complex graphs. However, it does not guarantee finding the shortest path between nodes, and it may get stuck in deep branches if the graph is infinite or cyclic.

3.4 GENERATE AND TEST ALGORITHM

The Generate and Test algorithm is a basic and intuitive problem-solving approach used in artificial intelligence and computer science. It is often employed when the problem space is relatively small or when the problem-solving process can be straightforwardly decomposed into two distinct stages:

generation and testing. The Generate and Test algorithm has been explained in Algorithm 3.

Algorithm 3 Generate and Test Algorithm

1. **Generation:** In the generation phase, potential solutions to the problem are generated systematically or randomly. This could involve generating all possible candidate solutions or sampling a subset of candidate solutions from the search space. The generation process typically produces a set of candidate solutions based on some predefined criteria or constraints.
2. **Testing:** In the testing phase, each generated solution is evaluated or tested against the problem's requirements or constraints. This involves checking whether each candidate solution satisfies the problem's criteria or meets the desired properties. The testing process typically involves applying a set of predefined rules, conditions, or evaluation functions to assess the quality or validity of each solution.
3. **Selection:** Depending on the problem requirements, a selection phase may follow the testing phase. In this phase, the best solution(s) among the tested candidates may be selected based on some optimization criteria (e.g., maximizing utility, minimizing cost).
4. **Termination:** The algorithm terminates once a satisfactory solution is found or after exploring all candidate solutions.

The Generate and Test algorithm is simple to implement and can be applied to a wide range of problems. However, it may not be the most efficient approach for large or complex problem spaces due to its exhaustive nature and lack of guidance in the search process. Additionally, it may not guarantee finding the optimal solution and may require significant computational resources if the search space is vast.

Despite its limitations, the Generate and Test algorithm remains a useful tool in situations where the problem space is relatively small, and a brute-force approach is feasible and sufficient to find satisfactory solutions. It is often used as a baseline or starting point for more sophisticated problem-solving techniques.

3.5 HILL CLIMBING ALGORITHM

The Hill Climbing algorithm is a basic optimization algorithm used in computer science and mathematical optimization. It belongs to the family of local search algorithms, which means it iteratively moves from one solution to another in the search space, gradually improving the quality of the solution until it reaches an optimal solution or a local maximum. Hill Climbing algorithm has been explained in Algorithm 4.

Algorithm 4 Hill Climbing Algorithm

1. **Initialization:** Start with an initial solution, which could be generated randomly or by some other means.
2. **Evaluation:** Evaluate the quality of the current solution using an objective function or fitness function. This function determines how good a solution is based on certain criteria. The objective is usually to maximize or minimize this function.
3. **Neighbor Generation:** Generate neighboring solutions by making small alterations to the current solution. These alterations can include small changes, additions, deletions, or swaps of elements depending on the problem.
4. **Selection:** Choose the best neighboring solution based on its evaluation using the objective function.
5. **Termination:** Repeat steps 3 and 4 until one of the termination conditions is met, such as reaching a maximum number of iterations, reaching a certain level of improvement, or reaching a solution that meets a predefined criterion.

The main idea behind Hill Climbing is to always move towards the direction of the steepest ascent (or descent, depending on the problem), continuously improving the solution at each step. While the Hill Climbing algorithm is straightforward and easy to implement, it does face several challenges, which can limit its effectiveness in certain scenarios. The major challenges of Hill Climbing algorithm are discussed below.

- **Local Optima:** One of the most significant challenges with Hill Climbing is its tendency to get trapped in local optima. If the search space has multiple peaks and valleys. Hill Climbing may converge to a suboptimal solution without exploring the entire space. This is particularly problematic in optimization problems where the objective function contains many local optima.
- **Plateaus and Ridges:** In some cases, the search space may contain plateaus or ridges where the objective function remains constant or changes very slowly. Hill Climbing can struggle to navigate such regions efficiently, leading to slow convergence or getting stuck altogether.
- **Greedy Nature:** Hill Climbing is a greedy algorithm that always moves to the neighboring solution with the best evaluation. While this approach is beneficial in many cases, it can also lead to premature convergence, where the algorithm settles for a solution that is locally optimal but not globally optimal.
- **Initial Solution Sensitivity:** The performance of Hill Climbing can be highly sensitive to the choice of the initial solution. If the initial

solution is far from the global optimum, the algorithm may require a large number of iterations or may never reach the optimal solution.

- **Computational Complexity:** While Hill Climbing is computationally efficient and scales well to large search spaces, its performance can degrade significantly when dealing with high-dimensional or continuous optimization problems. The increased complexity of evaluating neighboring solutions in such cases can slow down the convergence of the algorithm.
- **Lack of Memory:** Hill Climbing does not maintain a memory of previously visited solutions, which means it may revisit the same solutions multiple times, leading to inefficiencies during exploration.

To mitigate these challenges, various enhancements and modifications to the basic Hill Climbing algorithm have been proposed, including simulated annealing, genetic algorithms, and local beam search, among others. These variants introduce mechanisms to overcome local optima, introduce randomness to the search process, or maintain diversity in the explored solutions.

3.6 BEST FIRST SEARCH

Best First Search is an informed search algorithm used in the field of artificial intelligence. Unlike uninformed search algorithms like Breadth-First Search or Depth-First Search, Best First Search employs heuristics to guide the search process towards the most promising paths in the search space. It is commonly used in problems where the goal is to find the optimal path from a start node to a goal node in a graph or a search tree. Best First Search algorithm has been discussed in Algorithm 5.

Algorithm 5 Best First Search Algorithm

1. **Initialization:** Start with the initial node as the current node.
2. **Evaluation:** Evaluate the current node using a heuristic function, which estimates the cost or distance from the current node to the goal node. This heuristic function guides the search by providing information about which nodes are likely to lead to the goal.
3. **Expansion:** Expand the current node by generating its neighboring nodes (children) in the search space.
4. **Selection:** Select the most promising node among the generated nodes based on the heuristic function. This node becomes the new current node.
5. **Termination:** Repeat steps 2–4 until the goal node is found or until the search space is exhausted.

Let us understand working of Best First Search with the following example. Here, start state is 'A' and goal state is 'J'. The heuristic value for all the nodes 'A' to 'J' are as follows:

A-0, B-3, C-5, D-1, E-4, F-6, G-6, H-5, I-2, J-1

The search tree using best first search has been explained in Figure 3.1. The first move is from start node 'A' to node 'D', as node 'D' has the minimum heuristic value as compared to 'B' and 'C' at the same level. Now four nodes as 'B', 'C', 'E' and 'F' are possible, where 'B' has the minimum value and the next possibilities are 'G', 'H', 'C', 'E' and 'F'. As the node 'E' has the minimum value, its next nodes are 'I' and 'J'. The node 'J' is the goal node and algorithm terminates at this point, where goal state is met.

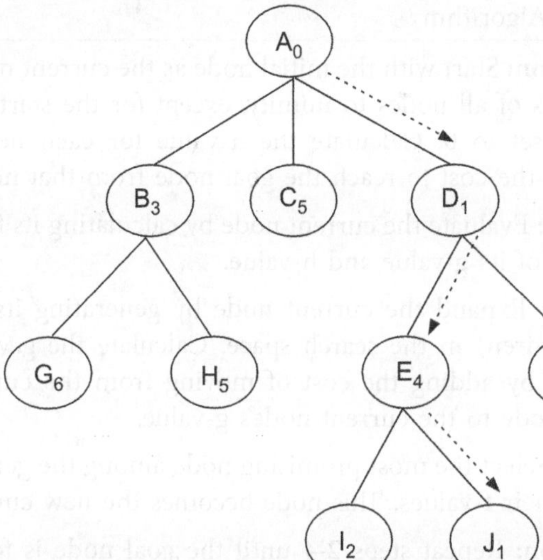

Figure 3.1 Best first search tree implementation.

The Best First Search relies heavily on the heuristic function, which provides an estimate of the cost from the current node to the goal node. The choice of heuristic function can significantly impact the performance and efficiency of the algorithm. A good heuristic function should be admissible (never overestimates the actual cost) and consistent (satisfies the triangle inequality). One common implementation of Best First Search is the A* algorithm, which uses both the heuristic function and the cost function (the actual cost of reaching the current node from the start node) to guide the search. A* is widely used due to its optimality (finding the optimal solution if one exists) and efficiency while using an admissible and consistent heuristic function. Overall, Best First Search algorithms are powerful tools for solving search and optimization problems, particularly in domains where heuristic information is available to guide the search process efficiently.

3.7 A* ALGORITHM

The A* algorithm is a widely used and well-known path finding algorithm in artificial intelligence. It is an extension of the Best First Search algorithm and is commonly used to find the shortest path from a start node to a goal node in a weighted graph or a grid. The key feature of A* is its ability to efficiently find the optimal path while exploring the search space by combining information about the cost to reach a node from the start node (known as "g-value") and a heuristic estimate of the cost from the node to the goal node (known as "h-value"). A* evaluates nodes based on a combination of these two values, aiming to minimize the sum of the g-value and h-value for each node. A* algorithm has been discussed in Algorithm 6.

Algorithm 6 A* Algorithm

1. **Initialization:** Start with the initial node as the current node. Initialize the g-values of all nodes to infinity, except for the start node, whose g-value is set to 0. Calculate the h-value for each node (heuristic estimate of the cost to reach the goal node from that node).
2. **Evaluation:** Evaluate the current node by calculating its f-value, which is the sum of its g-value and h-value.
3. **Expansion:** Expand the current node by generating its neighboring nodes (children) in the search space. Calculate the g-value for each child node by adding the cost of moving from the current node to the child node to the current node's g-value.
4. **Selection:** Select the most promising node among the generated nodes based on their f-values. This node becomes the new current node.
5. **Termination:** Repeat steps 2-4 until the goal node is found or until the search space is exhausted.

Let us understand the working of A* algorithm with following example. Here, start state is 'A' and goal state is 'E'. The heuristic value for all the nodes 'A' to 'E' are as follows:

A-4, B-5, C-2, D-1, E-0

In addition, cost values of edges between respective nodes are in A* search. The cost values of edges AB, AC, BC, BD, CD, BE and DE are 1, 4, 2, 5, 2, 12 and 3, respectively. The path with the least cost from 'A' to 'E' is 8 through AB-BC-CD-DE as compared to other paths between 'A' to 'E'.

The efficiency and optimality of the A* algorithm depend on the choice of heuristic function. A good heuristic function should be admissible (never overestimates the actual cost) and consistent (satisfies the triangle inequality). When an admissible and consistent heuristic function is used, A* guarantees to find the optimal path from the start node to the goal node. A* is widely used in various applications, including robotics, video games, network routing, and planning, where finding the shortest path efficiently is essential.

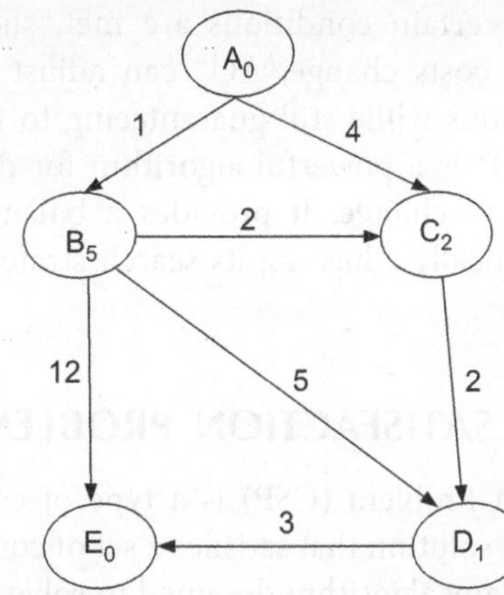

Figure 3.2 A* search tree implementation.

3.8 AO* ALGORITHM

The AO* (AO-star) algorithm is an extension of the A* algorithm, designed to handle environments with changing costs or dynamic environments. AO* stands for "Adaptive A*," as it dynamically adjusts its search based on the changing costs of traversing the graph or grid. In typical A* implementations, the cost associated with each edge in the graph remains fixed throughout the search process. However, in dynamic environments, these costs might change over time due to factors such as traffic congestion in route planning or changing terrain costs in robotics. The AO* algorithm has been explained in Algorithm 7.

Algorithm 7 AO* Algorithm

1. **Initialization:** Similar to A*, start with the initial node as the current node, and initialize the g-values of all nodes to infinity, except for the start node, whose g-value is set to 0.
2. **Evaluation:** Evaluate the current node by calculating its f-value, which is the sum of its g-value and h-value.
3. **Expansion:** Expand the current node by generating its neighboring nodes (children) in the search space. Calculate the g-value for each child node by adding the cost of moving from the current node to the child node to the current node's g-value.
4. **Selection:** Select the most promising node among the generated nodes based on their f-values. This node becomes the new current node.
5. **Termination:** Repeat steps 2–4 until the goal node is found or until the search space is exhausted.

However, in AO*, the algorithm periodically reassesses the costs and updates the search tree accordingly. It might do this after a certain number of expansions or when certain conditions are met, such as changes in the environment. When the costs change, AO* can adjust its search strategy to adapt to the new conditions while still guaranteeing to find the optimal path, if one exists. Overall, AO* is a powerful algorithm for dynamic environments where costs are subject to change. It provides a balance between efficiency and optimality by dynamically adjusting its search strategy based on changing conditions.

3.9 CONSTRAINT SATISFACTION PROBLEM

A Constraint Satisfaction Problem (CSP) is a type of computational problem where the goal is to find a solution that satisfies a set of constraints. A Constraint Satisfaction Algorithm is any algorithm designed to solve CSPs efficiently. These problems arise in various fields, including artificial intelligence, operations research, scheduling, and many others. Constraint Satisfaction Algorithm has been explained in Algorithm 8.

Algorithm 8 Constraint Satisfaction Problem Algorithm

1. **Representation:** The problem is represented in terms of variables, domains, and constraints.
2. **Variables:** Represent the entities to be assigned values.
3. **Domains:** Define the possible values that can be assigned to variables.
4. **Constraints:** Specify restrictions on the allowable combinations of values for sets of variables.
5. **Search:** The algorithm systematically searches through the space of possible assignments to variables to find a solution that satisfies all constraints. Various search strategies can be employed, such as backtracking, forward checking, or constraint propagation.
6. **Backtracking:** Backtracking is a commonly used technique for systematically searching through the space of possible solutions. At each step of the search, the algorithm selects a variable and tries all possible values from its domain, moving forward until either a solution is found or a constraint violation occurs.
7. **Constraint Propagation:** Constraint propagation techniques involve using the constraints to prune the search space, reducing the number of possible assignments that need to be considered. This can be done by enforcing local consistency, such as arc consistency or node consistency, to eliminate values from the domains of variables based on the constraints.
8. **Heuristics:** Heuristic techniques can be employed to guide the search process efficiently. This might involve selecting the most constrained variable (the variable with the fewest remaining values in its domain) or the variable involved in the most constraints first.

9. **Solution Checking:** Once a potential solution is found, it needs to be checked against all constraints to ensure that it satisfies all requirements. If the solution violates any constraint, the search continues to find an alternative solution.

The common examples of constraint satisfaction problems are letter digit constraints, N-Queens problem, Sudoku, map coloring, job scheduling, and many others. Constraint Satisfaction Algorithms provide a general framework for solving such problems efficiently by systematically exploring the space of possible solutions while respecting the specified constraints.

3.10 MEANS-END ANALYSIS

Means-End Analysis is a problem-solving technique used in artificial intelligence, cognitive psychology, and various other fields. It involves breaking down a problem into smaller subproblems and finding ways to reduce the difference between the current state and the desired goal state by applying operators or actions. The process involves repeatedly identifying the differences between the current state and the goal state, selecting an operator that can reduce or eliminate one of these differences, and applying the operator to move closer to the goal. This cycle continues until the current state matches the goal state. Means-End Analysis has been explained in Algorithm 9.

Algorithm 9 Means-End Analysis Algorithm

1. **Initial State:** Begin with the initial state of the problem, which represents the current situation or configuration.
2. **Goal State:** Identify the desired goal state that needs to be achieved.
3. **Difference Identification:** Analyze the differences between the current state and the goal state. These differences represent obstacles or barriers that need to be overcome to reach the goal.
4. **Operator Selection:** Select an operator or action that can reduce one of the identified differences. An operator is a transformation or action that can be applied to the current state to move closer to the goal state.
5. **Application of Operator:** Apply the selected operator to the current state, resulting in a new state.
6. **Goal Test:** Check if the new state matches the goal state. If yes, the problem is solved. If not, repeat steps 3–5 until the goal state is reached.

Means-End Analysis is often used in conjunction with other problem-solving techniques, such as heuristic search algorithms like A* or constraint satisfaction algorithms. It is particularly useful in domains where the problem space is large and complex, and breaking down the problem into smaller steps can help manage the complexity and guide the search for a solution. Overall,

Means-End Analysis provides a systematic approach to problem-solving by focusing on reducing the differences between the current state and the goal state, one step at a time.

EXERCISES

3.1 What are uninformed and informed searches? Differentiate with suitable examples.

3.2 How does blind search work? Discuss breadth-first search and depth-first search as blind search.

3.3 Write algorithms for breadth-first search and depth-first search.

3.4 Write breadth-first search and depth-first search computer programs, and discuss their complexities.

3.5 How is heuristic search helpful? Discuss a few cases where heuristic search solves problems easily.

3.6 List heuristic search examples.

3.7 Discuss algorithms for generate-and-test and hill climbing. What are the challenges in hill climbing?

3.8 Write computer programs for generate-and-test and hill climbing search.

3.9 Discuss the best first algorithm and its complexity.

3.10 Write a computer program for the best first search.

3.11 Discuss A* algorithm and its complexity.

3.12 Write a computer program for the A* algorithm.

3.13 Differentiate between best first search and A* algorithms.

3.14 Discuss AO* algorithm and its complexity.

3.15 Write a computer program for the AO* algorithm. How AO* algorithm performs better in selective cases?

3.16 What is the constraint satisfaction problem? Discuss its algorithm?

3.17 Solve constraint satisfaction problem for example (each character can have unique value as digit 0 to 9)

```
   SEND
 + MORE
 ------
  MONEY
```

3.18 Solve constraint satisfaction problem for example (each character can have unique value as digit 0 to 9)

```
   BASE
 + BALL
 ------
  GAMES
```

3.19 Discuss Means-End Analysis using suitable examples. How is this helpful in solving AI tasks?

3.20 Discuss transition tables for any example using Means-End Analysis approach.

CHAPTER 4

Knowledge Representation and Resolution Principle

4.1 KNOWLEDGE REPRESENTATION IN AI

Knowledge representation in AI refers to the methods and techniques used to encode, structure, and store information so that it can be effectively utilized by intelligent systems. Effective knowledge representation is crucial for enabling AI systems to reason, learn, and make decisions in various domains.

Some of the common approaches to knowledge representation in AI are listed as follows:

- **Logic-based Representation:** This approach represents knowledge using formal logic, such as propositional logic or first-order logic. Knowledge is encoded using logical symbols and rules, allowing for inference and reasoning. Knowledge bases, such as Semantic Networks, Frames, and Description Logics, are often used in this approach.
- **Semantic Networks:** Semantic networks represent knowledge in the form of nodes (concepts) and links (relationships) between them. They are often used to represent hierarchical structures and relationships between entities.
- **Frames:** Frames are similar to semantic networks but are more structured. They represent knowledge using a set of slots (attributes) and fillers (values), allowing for more detailed representations of objects or concepts.
- **Rule-based Systems:** In rule-based systems, knowledge is represented using a set of rules that encode relationships between different pieces of information. These rules can be used for pattern recognition, decision-making, and problem-solving.

The choice of knowledge representation depends on the specific requirements of the AI application and the nature of the problem being solved. Each approach has its advantages and limitations, and the selection often involves trade-offs between expressiveness, scalability, and computational efficiency.

4.2 LOGIC-BASED REPRESENTATION

Propositional logic and First Order Predicate Logic (FOPL) are two common types of logic-based representation. These are discussed in the following subsections.

4.2.1 Propositional Logic

Propositional logic is a branch of mathematical logic that deals with propositions, which are statements that can be either true or false. In propositional logic, these propositions are represented using symbols, and logical operations are performed on these symbols to derive conclusions. Common propositional logic elements are discussed here.

- **Propositions:** Propositions are statements that can be either true or false. They are represented using propositional variables, often denoted by letters, such as p, q, r etc. For example, "I am reading" can be represented as the proposition p, and "Today is a sunny day" can be represented as the proposition q.
- **Logical Connectives:** Logical connectives are symbols used to connect propositions and form compound propositions. The basic logical connectives in propositional logic are conjunction (logical AND), disjunction (logical OR), negation (logical NOT), implication (logical implication) and biconditional (logical equivalence).
  The conjunction symbol is $\wedge$, for proposition p and q, $p \wedge q$ is true if both p and q are true.
  The disjunction symbol is $\vee$, for proposition p and q, $p \vee q$ is true if atleast one of p or q is true.
  The negation symbol is $\neg$ and $\neg p$ is true, if p is false.
  The implication for p and q is, p implies q ($p \rightarrow q$). Here, $p \rightarrow q$ is true whenever p is true, q is also true.
  The biconditional is logical equivalence using symbol $\leftrightarrow$. For propositions p and q, $\leftrightarrow$ is true if p and q both are true.
- **Truth Tables:** Truth tables are used to enumerate all possible combinations of truth values for propositions and evaluate the truth value of compound propositions based on the truth values of their components. For example, truth table of $p \vee q$ is in Table 4.1.

Table 4.1 Truth table of $p \vee q$

p	q	$p \vee q$
T	T	T
T	F	T
F	T	T
F	F	F

- **Logical Equivalences:** Logical equivalences are relationships between compound propositions that have the same truth values under all possible truth value assignments to their components. Examples of logical equivalences include De Morgan's laws, distributive laws, and double negation.

4.2.2 First Order Predicate Logic

First Order Predicate Logic (FOPL) is a formal system in mathematical logic that extends propositional logic by introducing predicates, quantifiers, and variables. It allows for the formal representation and reasoning about statements involving objects and their properties. Predicates are expressions that can be true or false depending on the values of variables. They represent properties or relations that can be attributed to objects. For example, "Book cover is Red," "A is taller than B," "Kitty is a cat," etc. In FOPL, variables are symbols used to represent objects. For example, in the statement "x is taller than y," 'x' and 'y' are variables representing objects. The quantifiers specify the quantity of objects that satisfy a given predicate. The two main quantifiers are Universal Quantifier (∀) and existential quantifier (∃). The ∀ asserts that a statement holds for all objects in the domain. For example, $\forall x(P(x))$ means "for all x, $P(x)$ is true. The ∃ asserts that there exists at least one object in the domain for which a given statement is true. For example, $\exists x(P(x))$ means "there exists an x such that $P(x)$ is true." The FOPL include all elements of propositional logic, such as ∨, ∨, ¬, → and ←. These propositional components are connectives in predicate used to combine predicates and form more complex statements.

4.3 SEMANTIC NETWORKS

Semantic networks are graphical representations used to organize and represent knowledge in a way that reflects the meaning of concepts and the relationships between them. Nodes and links are two main components in a semantic network. Nodes represent concepts or entities. These can be objects, events, ideas, or any other meaningful unit of information. Links represent the relationships between concepts. These relationships can be of various types such as "is-a," "part-of," "causes," "related-to," etc. Each link has a specific meaning that defines the connection between the nodes it joins. Semantic networks are widely used in AI for tasks, such as natural language understanding, knowledge representation, and reasoning. They provide a structured way to capture and organize knowledge, enabling machines to understand and process information in a more human-like manner. One of the key advantages of semantic networks is their flexibility. They can easily accommodate new information by adding new nodes and links or modifying existing ones. This adaptability makes them valuable for building AI systems that can learn and evolve over time.

4.4 FRAMES

Frames provide a structured method for representing concepts, including their properties and relationships. The key components of a frame-based system are:

- **Frame:** A frame is a data structure that represents a specific concept or object. It consists of slots or attributes that describe various aspects of the concept, such as its properties, relationships, and behaviors. For example, a frame representing a car might have slots for its make, model, color, and year.
- **Slots:** Slots are the individual components of a frame that store specific pieces of information about the concept. Each slot has a name and may have a value associated with it. Slots can also have default values and constraints that define the valid range of values they can take.
- **Inheritance:** Frames can be organized in a hierarchical manner, with some frames inheriting properties and relationships from others. This allows for the representation of general concepts and their specialized instances. For example, a "Vehicle" frame may have slots such as "number of wheels" and "fuel type," which are inherited by more specific frames like "Car" and "Truck."
- **Frames and Scripts:** Frames can also represent typical sequences of events or actions, known as scripts. These are similar to frames but are used to represent stereotypical sequences of events, such as going to a restaurant or making a phone call.

Frame-based systems provide a way to represent complex knowledge in a structured and organized manner, making it easier for AI systems to understand and reason about the world. They have been used in various AI applications, including expert systems, natural language understanding, and knowledge representation. However, their rigid structure and reliance on predefined frames can also be a limitation, especially in domains where knowledge is constantly evolving or ambiguous.

4.5 RULE-BASED SYSTEMS

Rule-based systems encode knowledge in the form of rules, which consist of conditional statements that describe relationships between different pieces of information. Rule-based systems are widely used in various AI applications, including expert systems, decision support systems, and automated reasoning systems. The knowledge in a rule-based system is represented using a set of rules. Each rule typically has two parts, a condition (antecedent) and an action (consequent). The condition specifies a pattern or situation that must be satisfied for the rule to be applicable, while the action specifies what should be done if the condition is met. The other component, the inference engine is responsible for applying the rules to the available data or facts to draw conclusions or make decisions. It systematically matches the conditions of the rules against the current state of affairs and executes the actions of the rules whose conditions are satisfied. *M* component is Working Memory that stores the current state of the system, including the facts or data that are relevant to the problem domain. The inference engine accesses this working memory to evaluate the rules. Rule-based systems involve applying the rules to the working memory repeatedly until no more rules can be triggered or until a termination condition is met. During each cycle, the system may add new facts to the working memory, retract existing facts, or modify its internal state based on the actions specified in the rules. Transparency, modularity and inferencing are the key advantages of rule-based systems. However, brittleness, scalability and expressiveness are its limitations.

In addition, Ontologies, probabilistic models, connectionist models and hybrid approaches are also used in knowledge representation. Ontologies provide a formal representation of knowledge in a specific domain, including concepts, relationships, and constraints. They are often used to facilitate knowledge sharing and interoperability between different systems. In *probabilistic models*, knowledge is represented using probability distributions. This allows AI systems to deal with uncertainty and make decisions based on probabilistic reasoning. *Connectionist models*, such as artificial neural networks, represent knowledge using distributed representations across interconnected nodes. They are particularly effective for tasks involving pattern recognition and learning from data. *Hybrid Approaches* are the AI systems which combine multiple knowledge representation techniques to leverage their respective strengths. For example, a system might use a combination of logic-based representation for symbolic reasoning and connectionist models for pattern recognition.

4.6 RESOLUTION PRINCIPLE

The resolution principle is a key component of logical inference and theorem proving. The main steps in resolution principle are as follows:

- **Logical Inference:** Resolution is a rule of inference used in logic to derive new sentences from existing ones. It's particularly useful in automated reasoning systems where the goal is to automatically deduce conclusions from a set of premises.
- **Clausal Form:** Resolution operates on logical statements in clausal form, which is a standard representation in logic where each statement is expressed as a disjunction ($\vee$) of literals (atomic formulas or negated atomic formulas).
- **Resolution Rule:** The resolution rule states that if you have two clauses that contain complementary literals (a literal and its negation), then you can resolve them by eliminating those literals. The result is a new

clause formed by taking the union of the remaining literals from the two original clauses, excluding the complementary literals.
Example: Suppose for two clauses:
Clause 1: $A \vee B$
Clause 2: $\neg A \vee C$
By resolving these clauses on the literal A and its negation $\neg A$, the new clause is: $B \vee C$

- **Iterative Process:** Resolution is typically applied iteratively. You start with the given premises and repeatedly apply the resolution rule until either you derive the desired conclusion or you reach a point where no new clauses can be inferred.

Resolution is both sound and complete, which means that if there is a logical consequence of the given premises, resolution will eventually derive it. However, it may not always be efficient due to the potentially exponential growth of the search space. Resolution is widely used in automated theorem proving, logic programming (such as Prolog), and various AI systems for tasks like natural language understanding, planning, and problem-solving. The implementation of the resolution principle has been explained using Example 4.1.

For the following statements in Example 4.1:

1. Sachin likes all kinds of outdoor sports.
2. Cricket and Football are outdoor sports.
3. Any outdoor sport anyone plays and is not active is an outdoor sport.
4. Virat plays Hockey and is still active.
5. Shubham plays everything that Virat plays.

Now, based on the above statements, prove by resolution that:

Sachin likes Hockey.

The first step is to convert the above statements in FOPL. The respective FOPL statements are as follows (We have considered outdoor sport as 'sport' in this example):

1. $\forall x$: sport(x) $\rightarrow$ likes(Sachin, x)
2. sport(Cricket) $\wedge$ sport(Football)
3. $\forall x \forall y$: plays(x, y) $\wedge$ $\neg$inactive(x) $\rightarrow$ sport(y)
4. plays(Virat, Hockey) $\wedge$ active(Virat)
5. $\forall x$: plays(Virat,x) $\rightarrow$ plays(Shubham, x)
6. $\forall x$: $\neg$ inactive(x) $\rightarrow$ active(x)
7. $\forall x$: active(x) $\rightarrow$ $\neg$ inactive(x)
8. likes (Sachin, Hockey)

Here, statements 6 and 7 are added predicates and 8 is the statement to prove. The next step is to form a clause form for the above statements. This step mainly includes expansion of implication ($\rightarrow$) statements, move negation ($\neg$) inwards and standardize variables. The updated statements are as follows:

1. $\forall x : \neg \text{sport}(x) \vee \text{likes(Sachin}, x)$
2. $\text{sport(Cricket)} \wedge \text{sport(Football)}$
3. $\forall y, \forall z \neg \text{plays}(y, z) \vee \text{inactive}(y) \vee \text{sport}(z)$
4. $\text{plays(Virat, Hockey)} \wedge \text{active(Virat)}$
5. $\forall w, \neg \text{plays(Virat}, w) \vee \text{plays(Shubham}, w)$
6. $\forall g, \text{inactive}(g) \vee \text{active}(g)$
7. $\forall k, \neg \text{active}(k) \vee \neg \text{inactive}(k)$
8. likes(Sachin, Hockey)

Now, drop universal quantifiers as all the statements are not implicitly quantified. The updated statements are as follows:

1. $\neg \text{sport}(x) \vee \text{likes(Sachin}, x)$
2. $\text{sport(Cricket)} \wedge \text{sport(Football)}$
3. $\neg \text{plays}(y, z) \vee \text{inactive}(y) \vee \text{sport}(z)$
4. $\text{plays(Virat, Hockey)} \wedge \text{active(Virat)}$
5. $\neg \text{plays(Virat}, w) \vee \text{plays(Shubham}, w)$
6. $\text{inactive}(g) \vee \text{active}(g)$
7. $\neg \text{active}(k) \vee \neg \text{inactive}(k)$
8. likes(Sachin, Hockey)

Now, the last step includes, negate the statement to be proved and if output is *null*, the claim is true. This has been demonstrated using resolution graph in Figure 4.1. The output in Figure 4.1 is Φ, which proves the statement "Sachin likes Hockey".

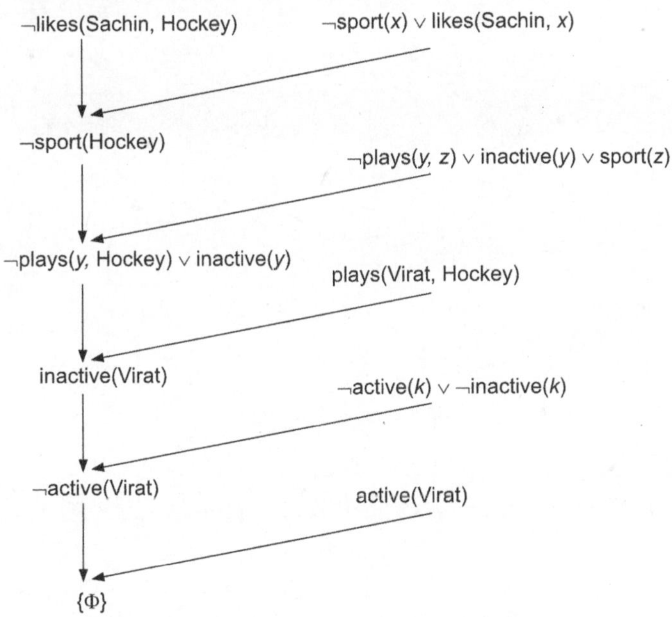

Figure 4.1 Resolution graph for Example 4.1.

EXERCISES

4.1 What is knowledge representation? Discuss various approaches of knowledge representation.

4.2 List the advantages and disadvantages of logic-based representation.

4.3 Discuss few examples of propositional and predicate logic.

4.4 How semantic networks help in knowledge representation? Write an example of semantic network for knowledge representation.

4.5 Write short note on frames with examples.

4.6 How rule-based systems are applied? Discuss with an example.

4.7 What is clause form? Give examples.

4.8 Discuss resolution principle with an example.

CHAPTER 5

Expert Systems

5.1 KEY FEATURES OF EXPERT SYSTEMS

In the realm of AI, an expert system represents a specific application or approach. It's a type of AI system designed to replicate the decision-making ability of a human expert in a particular domain. The key features of expert system are as follows:

- **Domain Expertise:** Expert systems excel in domains where human expertise is crucial. These could include fields such as medicine, finance, engineering, and troubleshooting complex systems. By capturing the knowledge and decision-making processes of human experts, these systems can provide valuable insights and recommendations.
- **Knowledge Representation:** Expert systems store their knowledge in a structured format known as a knowledge base. This knowledge base contains information about the domain, including facts, rules, and heuristics derived from human experts. The knowledge is typically encoded using symbolic representations that the system can interpret and manipulate.
- **Inference Engine:** The inference engine is the reasoning component of an expert system. It uses the knowledge stored in the knowledge base to make inferences and draw conclusions about specific problems or situations. This involves applying logical rules, pattern matching, and reasoning algorithms to arrive at solutions.
- **Rule-based Reasoning:** Expert systems often employ a rule-based approach to reasoning, where decision rules are represented as "if-then" statements. These rules encode the conditions under which certain actions or conclusions should be taken. The inference engine evaluates these rules based on the input data and the current state of the problem to derive appropriate responses.
- **Explanation Facility:** Many expert systems include an explanation facility to provide users with insights into the system's decision-

making process. This transparency helps users understand why certain recommendations are made and builds trust in the system's capabilities. Explanations may involve tracing the reasoning steps taken by the system or highlighting the rules that influenced the outcome.

- **User Interaction:** Expert systems often feature user interfaces that allow users to interact with the system, input data, and receive recommendations. These interfaces can vary in complexity, ranging from command-line interfaces to graphical user interfaces (GUIs) with interactive visualization tools. Effective user interaction is essential for enabling users to leverage the system's capabilities efficiently.
- **Learning and Adaptation:** Some expert systems incorporate learning mechanisms to improve their performance over time. These systems may analyze feedback from users or new data to refine their knowledge base and decision-making algorithms. By continuously learning from experience, expert systems can adapt to changing conditions and improve their accuracy and effectiveness.

Despite their strengths, expert systems have limitations. They may struggle with tasks that require tacit knowledge, intuition, or complex reasoning beyond the scope of explicit rules. Additionally, expert systems may not handle uncertainty, ambiguity, or novel situations well, which can limit their applicability in dynamic or unpredictable environments.

Overall, expert systems represent a powerful approach to leveraging human expertise in AI applications. By capturing and codifying domain knowledge, these systems can provide valuable decision support and problem-solving capabilities across a wide range of domains.

5.2 EXPERT SYSTEM ARCHITECTURE

The architecture of an expert system typically comprises several interconnected components that work together to achieve the system's objectives. Key components of expert system architecture are discussed here and expert system block diagram shown in Figure 5.1.

- **Knowledge Base (KB):** The knowledge base is the central component of an expert system, containing all the domain-specific knowledge and expertise. It includes facts, rules, heuristics, procedures, and any other relevant information about the problem domain. The knowledge is typically represented in a structured format that the system can interpret and manipulate, such as production rules, frames, semantic networks, or ontologies.
- **Inference Engine (IE):** The inference engine is responsible for reasoning and decision-making based on the knowledge stored in the knowledge base. It interprets user queries or problems and uses

inference mechanisms to derive conclusions or recommendations. The inference engine applies various reasoning strategies, such as forward chaining, backward chaining, or a combination of both, to reach solutions.

- **User Interface (UI):** The user interface allows users to interact with the expert system, input queries or problems, and receive outputs or recommendations. Depending on the application, the user interface may include text-based interfaces, graphical user interfaces (GUIs), command-line interfaces, or even natural language interfaces. An intuitive and user-friendly interface is essential for facilitating effective communication between the user and the system.
- **Explanation Facility:** Many expert systems include an explanation facility to provide users with insights into the system's decision-making process. The explanation facility explains how the system arrived at a particular conclusion or recommendation, helping users understand the reasoning behind the system's outputs. Explanations may involve tracing the inference steps taken by the system, highlighting the rules or knowledge used, or providing examples and justifications.
- **Knowledge Acquisition (KA):** Knowledge acquisition is the process of acquiring, eliciting, and encoding domain knowledge into the knowledge base. It involves interactions with domain experts, domain analysis, knowledge elicitation techniques, and knowledge representation methods. The knowledge acquisition component may include tools and methods to facilitate the acquisition and maintenance of knowledge within the system.
- **Knowledge Refinement and Learning:** Some expert systems incorporate mechanisms for knowledge refinement and learning over time. These mechanisms enable the system to improve its performance by analyzing feedback from users, updating the knowledge base, and refining its inference strategies. Learning techniques may include machine learning algorithms, data mining methods, or expert-guided refinement processes.
- **Control Component:** The control component coordinates the interactions between the various components of the expert system. It manages the flow of control, data, and communication within the system, ensuring that all components work together effectively. The control component may include mechanisms for task scheduling, resource allocation, error handling, and system monitoring.

Overall, the architecture of an expert system is designed to encapsulate and utilize domain expertise effectively, enabling the system to provide intelligent decision support and problem-solving capabilities in specific domains.

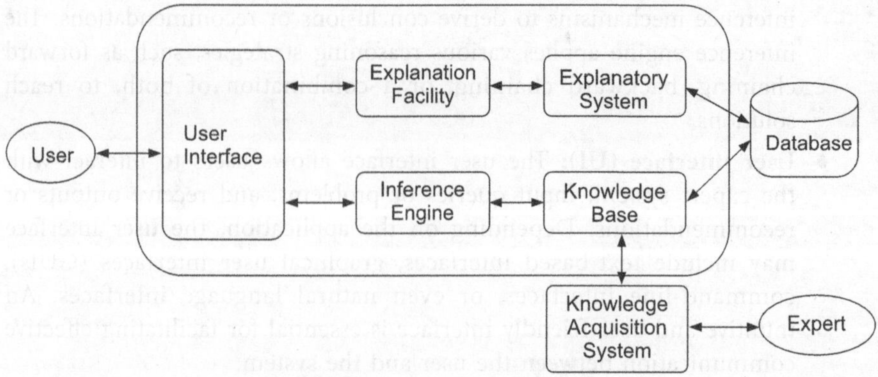

Figure 5.1 Expert system block diagram.

5.3 EXPERT SYSTEM EXAMPLES

Expert systems have been deployed in various domains to provide decision support and problem-solving capabilities. Some of the selected expert systems are discussed below.

- **MYCIN:** Developed in the 1970s, MYCIN was one of the earliest expert systems designed to assist physicians in diagnosing infectious diseases and recommending antibiotic treatments based on patient symptoms and laboratory test results.
- **LPA (Loan Production Assistant):** LPA is an expert system used in the banking industry to evaluate loan applications. It analyzes financial data, credit history, and risk factors to assess the creditworthiness of applicants and recommend loan approval or rejection.
- **DENDRAL:** Developed in the 1960s, DENDRAL was an expert system used for chemical analysis and molecular structure determination. It analyzed mass spectrometry data to identify organic compounds and propose molecular structures.
- **XCON:** XCON was an expert system developed by Digital Equipment Corporation (DEC) in the 1980s to configure and troubleshoot computer systems. It guided technicians through the process of diagnosing hardware and software issues and recommending solutions.
- **R1:** R1 is an expert system used by IBM to provide technical support for their hardware products. It assists support technicians in diagnosing problems, identifying solutions, and guiding customers through troubleshooting procedures.
- **Carnegie Mellon University's Cognitive Tutors:** Cognitive Tutors are expert systems designed to provide personalized tutoring and feedback to students in various subjects, such as mathematics and science.

They adapt to each student's learning pace and style, offering tailored instruction and practice exercises.

- **LEX:** LEX is an expert system used in the legal domain to provide assistance with legal research, case analysis, and decision-making. It helps legal professionals identify relevant laws, precedents, and arguments to support their cases.
- **PROSPECTOR:** PROSPECTOR is an expert system used in the mining industry to analyze geological data and identify potential locations of mineral deposits. It combines geological knowledge with statistical analysis to make predictions about the presence of valuable minerals.

These examples demonstrate the versatility and applicability of expert systems across diverse domains, where they leverage human expertise to provide intelligent decision support and problem-solving capabilities. Today, the list of expert systems is very long and the readers are encouraged to explore the recent applications of expert system.

5.4 NATURAL LANGUAGE PROCESSING

Natural Language Processing (NLP) is a subfield of artificial intelligence and linguistics concerned with the interactions between computers and human languages. It focuses on enabling computers to understand, interpret, and generate human language in a way that is both meaningful and contextually appropriate. The common tasks of NLP include text processing, language understanding, language generation, grammatical understanding etc.

The text processing in NLP involves various techniques for processing and manipulating text data. This includes tasks such as tokenization (breaking text into words or sentences), stemming and lemmatization (reducing words to their root forms), and part-of-speech tagging (identifying the grammatical parts of words). In language understanding, NLP aims to enable computers to understand the meaning and intent behind human language. This involves tasks such as named entity recognition (identifying entities, such as people, organizations, or locations mentioned in text), sentiment analysis (determining the sentiment or emotion expressed in text), and semantic analysis (extracting the meaning of text in context). The language generation in NLP involves techniques for generating human-like language. This includes tasks, such as machine translation (translating text from one language to another), text summarization (producing concise summaries of longer texts) and text generation (creating new text based on given prompts or contexts).

The Syntax and Grammar: Understanding the syntactic and grammatical structure of language is crucial in NLP. Techniques such as parsing (analyzing the grammatical structure of sentences) and dependency parsing (identifying the relationships between words in a sentence) are used to extract structural information from text.

Today, NLP applications are quite popular and growing rapidly. The virtual assistants and chatbots for natural language interaction; information retrieval and search engines for finding relevant documents or web pages; text analysis for social media monitoring, customer feedback analysis, and market research; language translation and localization for multilingual communication; text-to-speech and speech-to-text systems for voice interfaces and accessibility tools are popular applications.

5.5 NLP STAGES

There are five general stages or steps that are often followed in the processing pipeline of NLP. These are discussed as follows.

- **Text Preprocessing:** This stage involves cleaning and preparing the raw text data for further analysis. Tasks in this stage mainly include tokenization, removing noise, normalization, stopword removal and, stemming etc. The tokenization break text into smaller units such as words or phrases. Removing noise removes irrelevant information such as punctuation, special characters, and HTML tags. The normalization standardize text by converting it to lowercase, removing accents, and expanding contractions. Stopword removal remove common words (e.g., "and", "the", "is") that often carry little semantic meaning. Lemmatization or stemming reduce words to their base or root form to consolidate variations of the same word.
- **Text Representation:** In this stage, text data is transformed into a format suitable for computational analysis. Common techniques for text representation include bag-of-words, term frequency-inverse document frequency and, word embedding etc. Bag-of-Words represents text as a matrix where rows correspond to documents and columns correspond to unique words, with each cell containing a count or frequency of a word in the corresponding document.The term frequency-inverse document frequency assign weights to words based on their frequency in a document relative to their frequency in the entire corpus. Word embedding represents words as dense vectors in a continuous vector space, capturing semantic relationships between words.
- **Feature Engineering:** This stage involves selecting or generating features that are relevant for the NLP task at hand. Depending on the task, features may include N-grams, word embedding, syntactic features domain specific features, etc. N-grams are sequences of adjacent words or characters. Pre-trained word embeddings or custom word embeddings capture semantic meaning. Syntactic features are based on linguistic structures such as part-of-speech tags or syntax trees. While domain-specific features are tailored to the specific domain or application of the NLP task.

- **Model Building:** In this stage, machine learning or deep learning models are trained on the prepared text data to perform the desired NLP task. Common models used in NLP include classification models, sequence-to-sequence models, clustering models etc. Classification models (e.g., logistic regression, support vector machines, neural networks) work well for tasks, such as sentiment analysis, text classification, and named entity recognition. Sequence-to-sequence models (e.g., recurrent neural networks, transformers) for machine translation, text summarization, and question answering. And clustering models (e.g., k-means clustering, hierarchical clustering) for tasks like topic modeling and document clustering.
- **Evaluation and Deployment:** In this final stage, the performance of the trained model is evaluated using appropriate metrics to assess its effectiveness. Depending on the task, evaluation metrics may include accuracy, precision, recall, F1-score, or others. Once the model meets the desired performance criteria, it can be deployed into production environments for real-world applications.

These stages provide a structured framework for developing NLP solutions, but the specific steps and techniques employed may vary depending on the task, data, and available resources.

EXERCISES

5.1 What is expert system? Discuss key features of expert system.

5.2 How knowledge representation and inference engine are important for expert system? Give examples.

5.3 What is explanation facility in expert system? What could be the impact on system if we remove this feature.

5.4 How user interface is an important facility in expert system? What are the challenges if we ignore user interface?

5.5 Discuss expert system architecture in detail.

5.6 Give block diagram of expert system and explain its components.

5.7 List few expert system-based applications and their uses in our real life.

5.8 What is NLP? Write a short note on NLP advantages in our real life.

5.9 Discuss NLP process in detail. Mention atleast five major steps used in NLP working.

5.10 List sequential order for the stages of NLP designing.

5.11 What are key advantages of NLP? What could be the challenges of NLP in our real life tasks?

5.12 List few applications which are based on NLP.

CHAPTER 6

Soft Computing

6.1 KEY COMPONENTS OF SOFT COMPUTING

Soft computing is a branch of computer science that deals with approximate solutions to complex problems. Unlike traditional computing techniques, which rely on precise mathematical models and algorithms, soft computing approaches are tolerant to uncertainty, imprecision, and partial truth. Soft computing techniques often draw inspiration from human-like reasoning and decision-making processes. The key components of soft computing include neural networks, fuzzy logic, evolutionary computation and probabilistic reasoning.

- **Neural Networks** are computational models inspired by the structure and function of the human brain. They are used for tasks, such as pattern recognition, classification, and prediction, and are capable of learning from data.
- **Fuzzy Logic** deals with reasoning that is approximate rather than exact. It allows for the representation of imprecise or vague information by assigning degrees of truth to statements.
- **Evolutionary Computation Techniques** are inspired by the process of natural selection and genetics. They include genetic algorithms, evolutionary programming, and genetic programming, which are used for optimization and search problems.
- **Probabilistic Reasoning** involves dealing with uncertainty by representing and reasoning with probabilities. Techniques such as Bayesian networks and probabilistic graphical models are used for this purpose.

In addition, hybrid systems are other types of soft computing where more than one soft computing techniques properties are implemented together. Soft computing techniques are particularly useful in situations where problems are complex, poorly defined, or involve incomplete information. They have applications in various fields including artificial intelligence, control systems, optimization, data mining, and decision support systems.

6.2 NEURAL NETWORKS

Neural networks are computational models inspired by the structure and function of the human brain. Neural networks consist of interconnected nodes, called neurons, organized into layers. Each neuron receives inputs, processes them, and produces an output that is passed on to other neurons. Neural networks are trained using large amounts of data to perform tasks such as pattern recognition, classification, regression, and more. The common components or features of neural networks are listed below. Whereas, the neural networks has been explained, in details, in the subsequent chapters.

- **Neurons:** These are the basic processing units in a neural network. Each neuron receives input signals, applies a transformation (usually involving a weighted sum and an activation function), and produces an output signal.
- **Layers:** The neurons in a neural network are typically organized into layers. The most common types of layers are input layer (receives input data and passes it to the next layer), hidden layer (intermediate layers between the input and output layers which perform computations to extract features from the input data), and output layer (produces the final output of the network).
- **Weights and Biases:** Neural networks learn by adjusting the weights and biases associated with each connection between neurons. These parameters determine the strength of the connections and influence the output of each neuron.
- **Activation Functions:** Activation functions introduce non-linearities into the network, allowing it to learn complex patterns in the data. Common activation functions include sigmoid, tanh, ReLU (Rectified Linear Unit), and softmax.
- **Forward Propagation:** This is the process of passing input data through the network to generate predictions. Each layer applies transformations to the input data, propagating it forward until the output layer produces a prediction.
- **Backpropagation:** In neural networks, backpropagation is the process used to train neural networks. It involves computing the error between the predicted output and the actual target, then propagating this error backward through the network to update the weights and biases using optimization algorithms such as gradient descent.
- **Training Data:** Neural networks require large amounts of labeled training data to learn meaningful representations from the input data. The training data consists of input-output pairs used to adjust the network's parameters during training.

Neural networks have demonstrated remarkable success in various fields, including computer vision, natural language processing, speech recognition, medical diagnosis, and autonomous vehicles. Their ability to learn complex patterns from data makes them powerful tools for solving a wide range of tasks.

6.3 FUZZY LOGIC

Fuzzy logic is a form of logic that deals with reasoning and decision-making in the presence of uncertainty, imprecision, and vagueness. Unlike traditional binary logic, which operates on the principles of true or false, fuzzy logic allows for the representation of partial truths and degrees of membership. It is particularly useful in situations where the boundaries between categories are fuzzy or where precise numerical values are difficult to define. The key concepts of fuzzy logic are listed below:

- **Fuzzy Sets:** In fuzzy logic, sets are not defined by strict membership criteria but by degrees of membership. An element can belong to a set to a certain degree, ranging from fully belonging (1) to not belonging at all (0). This degree of membership is often represented by a membership function, which assigns a value between 0 and 1 to each element of the set.
- **Fuzzy Logic Operations:** These operations are AND, OR, and NOT generalized to handle fuzzy sets. For example, the fuzzy AND operation between two fuzzy sets results in a new fuzzy set representing the degree of overlap between the two sets.
- **Fuzzy Rules and Inference:** Fuzzy logic uses fuzzy rules to model human reasoning. These rules take the form of "IF-THEN" statements, where the "IF" part specifies conditions using fuzzy sets, and the "THEN" part specifies conclusions. Fuzzy inference combines these rules to produce a fuzzy output from fuzzy inputs.
- **Membership Functions:** Membership functions define how each input variable contributes to the output of a fuzzy logic system. They describe the degree to which input values belong to each fuzzy set.
- **Fuzzification and Defuzzification:** Fuzzification involves the conversion of crisp values to fuzzy values using fuzzy sets, membership functions, and fuzzification techniques, such as inference, intuition, maxima or minima, etc. Defuzzification is the process of converting fuzzy outputs into crisp values or actions. Various methods, such as centroid defuzzification or maximum membership defuzzification, are used in this phase.

Fuzzy logic has applications in various fields, including control systems, decision support systems, expert systems, pattern recognition and artificial intelligence. It is particularly well-suited for tasks that involve human-like reasoning, handling imprecise data or dealing with ambiguous or uncertain information. Fuzzy logic provides a flexible framework for modeling complex systems and making decisions in real-world scenarios where traditional binary logic may fall short.

6.4 EVOLUTIONARY COMPUTATION

Evolutionary computation is a problem-solving technique inspired by the principles of biological evolution. It is a subfield of artificial intelligence and computational intelligence. The basic idea is to mimic the process of natural selection to solve optimization and search problems. The common processes of evolutionary computation are discussed below.

- **Initialization:** A population of candidate solutions is generated randomly or using some heuristic method.
- **Evaluation:** Each candidate solution is evaluated against some predefined criteria, usually by assigning a fitness score.
- **Selection:** Solutions are selected to undergo genetic operations (such as crossover and mutation) based on their fitness scores. This mimics the natural selection process, where fitter individuals are more likely to pass on their genes to the next generation.
- **Reproduction:** Selected solutions are combined through genetic operators to produce offspring. Crossover involves exchanging genetic information between solutions, while mutation introduces random changes.
- **Replacement:** The offspring population replaces the previous generation, either entirely or partially.
- **Termination:** The process continues for a predefined number of generations or until a termination criterion is met.

The main advantage of evolutionary computation lies in its ability to explore large solution spaces and find near-optimal solutions in complex, multi-dimensional problem domains where traditional methods may struggle. Evolutionary algorithms, such as genetic algorithms, evolutionary strategies, and genetic programming, have been successfully applied to various domains, including optimization, machine learning, robotics and design automation.

6.4.1 Genetic Algorithms

Genetic Algorithms (GAs) are a type of evolutionary algorithm that simulates the process of natural selection to solve optimization and search problems. They are inspired by the principles of natural selection and genetics. The common stages in GA are initialization, evaluation, selection, recombination (crossover), mutation, replacement, and termination. The details are discussed in Chapters 12. Genetic algorithms have been successfully applied to a wide range of optimization and search problems, including function optimization, scheduling, routing, machine learning, and many others. They offer advantages such as robustness, ability to handle non-linear and non-differentiable objective functions, and suitability for parallel and distributed computing environments.

6.5 PROBABILISTIC REASONING

Probabilistic reasoning in soft computing involves dealing with uncertainty using probabilistic models and techniques. Soft computing encompasses various computational paradigms that handle imprecision, uncertainty and partial truth, and probabilistic reasoning plays a crucial role in addressing uncertainty within this framework. The key parts of probabilistic reasoning are listed below.

- **Probability Theory:** Soft computing approaches often utilize probability theory as a mathematical framework to represent and reason about uncertainty. Probabilistic models, such as Bayesian networks, Markov models, and probabilistic graphical models are employed to capture uncertain relationships between variables.
- **Bayesian Inference:** Bayesian inference is a fundamental technique in soft computing that allows updating beliefs or making predictions in the presence of uncertainty. It combines prior knowledge with observed data to compute the posterior distribution over unknown quantities of interest.
- **Probabilistic Graphical Models:** Soft computing often employs probabilistic graphical models (PGMs) to represent complex probabilistic relationships between variables. PGMs, such as Bayesian networks and Markov networks, provide a graphical representation of dependencies among variables and enable efficient probabilistic inference.
- **Uncertainty Quantification:** Soft computing techniques incorporate probabilistic reasoning to quantify uncertainty in decision-making processes. Uncertainty quantification methods assess the confidence or reliability of predictions or decisions by estimating uncertainty bounds or confidence intervals.
- **Machine Learning and Data Mining:** Soft computing techniques, including probabilistic reasoning, are widely used in machine learning and data mining applications. Probabilistic models, such as probabilistic graphical models and Bayesian classifiers are utilized for tasks such as classification, regression, clustering, and pattern recognition in the presence of uncertainty.

Probabilistic reasoning plays a vital role in soft computing by providing effective methods to model, reason about, and handle uncertainty, which is inherent in many real-world problems. Integrating probabilistic techniques with soft computing paradigms enables more robust and adaptive systems capable of dealing with complex and uncertain environments.

6.6 HYBRID SYSTEMS

Hybrid systems in soft computing refer to the integration of multiple computational paradigms or techniques to solve complex problems. Soft computing itself is characterized by its ability to handle uncertainty, imprecision, and partial truth, and hybrid systems leverage this flexibility by combining different soft computing approaches synergistically. Some of the examples of hybrid systems in soft computing are discussed here.

- **Fuzzy-Neural Systems:** Combining fuzzy logic with neural networks forms a powerful hybrid system. Fuzzy logic handles linguistic uncertainty and imprecision, while neural networks are adept at learning from data and capturing complex patterns. Fuzzy neural systems have been used for tasks such as control systems, pattern recognition, and prediction.
- **Evolutionary Fuzzy Systems:** Evolutionary algorithms, such as genetic algorithms or evolutionary strategies, are combined with fuzzy logic to create evolutionary fuzzy systems. These systems use evolutionary computation to optimize fuzzy logic systems' parameters or structures, enabling automated design and tuning of fuzzy systems.
- **Fuzzy-Genetic Algorithms:** Genetic algorithms are integrated with fuzzy logic to form fuzzy-genetic algorithms. Fuzzy logic is used to handle imprecise or uncertain fitness evaluations in genetic algorithms, guiding the search process more effectively, particularly in optimization problems with fuzzy objectives or constraints.
- **Hybrid Bayesian Networks:** Bayesian networks, probabilistic graphical models that represent probabilistic relationships among variables, can be enhanced with fuzzy logic or neural networks. This integration allows for the modeling of uncertain relationships between variables using fuzzy or neural representations within the Bayesian framework.
- **Neuro-Evolutionary Optimization:** Evolutionary algorithms, such as genetic algorithms or differential evolution, are combined with neural networks to create neuro-evolutionary optimization systems. Neural networks is used to guide the evolutionary search process or to incorporate fuzzy constraints or objectives into the optimization problem.

These hybrid systems leverage the complementary strengths of different soft computing techniques to tackle complex problems more effectively, often achieving better performance, robustness, and interpretability than individual approaches alone. By integrating multiple paradigms, hybrid systems in soft computing can address a broader range of challenges across various domains, including engineering, finance, healthcare, and more.

6.7 APPLICATIONS OF SOFT COMPUTING

Soft computing finds applications across various domains due to its ability to deal with uncertainty, imprecision, and complexity. Here are some common applications of soft computing techniques mentioned below.

- **Pattern Recognition and Image Processing:** Soft computing methods like neural networks, fuzzy logic, and evolutionary algorithms are widely used in pattern recognition tasks, such as handwriting recognition, facial recognition, object detection, and image classification.
- **Control Systems:** Soft computing techniques are applied in control systems for modeling, identification, and control of complex dynamic systems. Fuzzy logic controllers, neural network controllers, and adaptive control systems based on evolutionary algorithms are used in industrial automation, robotics, and process control.
- **Data Mining and Machine Learning:** Soft computing methods play a crucial role in data mining and machine learning tasks, including classification, clustering, regression, and anomaly detection. Neural networks, genetic algorithms, fuzzy clustering, and support vector machines are commonly used in these applications.
- **Predictive Modeling:** Soft computing techniques are utilized in predictive modeling tasks, such as weather forecasting, stock market prediction, demand forecasting, and predictive maintenance. Neural networks and fuzzy systems can capture complex patterns in historical data to make accurate predictions.
- **Bioinformatics and Computational Biology:** Soft computing methods are employed in bioinformatics and computational biology for tasks, such as protein structure prediction, gene expression analysis, drug discovery, and genomics data analysis. Neural networks, genetic algorithms, and evolutionary computation techniques are applied to analyze biological data and solve complex biological problems.
- **Financial Forecasting and Trading:** Soft computing techniques are used in financial forecasting and trading applications to analyze market data, predict stock prices, and optimize trading strategies. Neural networks, genetic algorithms, and fuzzy systems are employed to model financial data and make trading decisions.
- **Automated Diagnosis and Decision Support Systems:** Soft computing methods are applied in healthcare for automated diagnosis, medical image analysis, and decision support systems. Neural networks, fuzzy logic, and evolutionary algorithms are used to analyze patient data, assist in medical diagnosis, and provide personalised treatment recommendations.
- **Robotics and Autonomous Systems:** Soft computing techniques play a crucial role in robotics and autonomous systems for perception,

planning, and control. Neural networks, fuzzy logic, and evolutionary algorithms are used to develop intelligent robots capable of navigating environments, performing tasks, and learning from experience.

- **Natural Language Processing:** Soft computing methods are employed in natural language processing tasks such as sentiment analysis, language translation, and speech recognition. Neural networks, recurrent neural networks, and deep learning techniques are used to process and understand human language.
- **Optimization and Decision Making:** Soft computing techniques are applied in optimization and decision-making problems across various domains, including engineering, logistics, and scheduling. Genetic algorithms, particle swarm optimization, and fuzzy decision-making systems are used to find optimal solutions in complex, uncertain, and dynamic environments.

These applications demonstrate the versatility and effectiveness of soft computing techniques in solving real-world problems across diverse domains. Soft computing continues to evolve and find new applications as researchers develop innovative algorithms and methodologies to address emerging challenges.

EXERCISES

6.1 What is soft computing and how is it different from traditional computing?

6.2 Why soft computing is called approximate computing? List a few examples to support your claim.

6.3 Discuss atleast three types of soft computing.

6.4 What are neural network characteristics? Explain.

6.5 What are fuzzy logic characteristics? Explain.

6.6 What are evolutionary computation characteristics? Explain.

6.7 How are genetic algorithms different from neural networks and fuzzy logic? Is it an evolutionary technique? Justify.

6.8 List the properties of genetic algorithm.

6.9 What is probabilistic reasoning. Discuss in detail.

6.10 What are the advantages of hybrid systems? Discuss few examples.

6.11 Why neuro-fuzzy and fuzzy-genetic are hybrid systems? Discuss with examples.

6.12 List some real life applications based on hybrid systems.

6.13 Discuss the applications of hybrid system.

6.14 Write a short note on Bayesian models in context of soft computing.

6.15 How are machine learning techniques related to soft computing properties? Explain.

CHAPTER 7

Artificial Neural Networks

7.1 INTRODUCTION

Artificial Neural Networks (ANNs) are computational models inspired by the structure and function of biological neural networks in the human brain. They are a fundamental component of machine learning and artificial intelligence. ANNs consist of interconnected nodes, called neurons or units, organized into layers. The main components of ANNs are neurons; input, hidden and output layers; weights, biases, activation function, backpropagation, and loss functions. Artificial neural networks have been successfully applied to various tasks, including image recognition, natural language processing, speech recognition, and many others. Their ability to learn complex patterns from data makes them powerful tools for solving a wide range of real-world problems.

The history of ANNs dates back to the 1940s, and it has seen several key milestones and developments over the decades. The McCulloch-Pitts Neuron Model in 1943 was the earliest concept of an artificial neurons, which was proposed by Warren McCulloch and Walter Pitts. They introduced a mathematical model that mimicked the basic functioning of a biological neuron, laying the foundation for later developments in ANNs. In 1957, perceptron developed by Frank Rosenblatt was one of the earliest types of artificial neural networks. It consisted of a single layer of neurons with adjustable weights and was capable of learning simple patterns. However, its limitations in handling non-linear problems and inability to solve XOR-type problems led to a decline in interest in ANNs during the 1960s and 1970s. In the late 1970s and early 1980s, the backpropagation algorithm was independently rediscovered by multiple researchers, including Paul Werbos, David Rumelhart, Geoffrey Hinton, and Ronald Williams. Backpropagation revolutionized neural network training by allowing for efficient adjustment of network parameters to minimize error. This led to renewed interest in ANNs and sparked the development of more sophisticated network architectures and learning algorithms. With the development of backpropagation, multi-layer perceptrons (MLPs) in 1980s became feasible. MLPs consist of multiple layers of neurons, allowing them to learn complex non-linear relationships in data. This architecture became a cornerstone of neural network research and applications. The Support Vector

Machines (SVMs) and other techniques emerged in the 1990s. While neural networks continued to develop, other machine learning techniques such as SVMs gained popularity due to their efficiency and effectiveness, particularly in classification tasks. This period saw a diversification of machine learning methods and competition among different approaches. The 2000s witnessed a resurgence of interest in deep learning, fueled by advances in computing power, the availability of large-scale datasets, and improvements in neural network architectures and training algorithms. Deep learning, particularly deep neural networks with many hidden layers, has achieved remarkable success in various domains, including computer vision, natural language processing, speech recognition, and more. The Convolutional Neural Networks (CNNs) is a type of deep neural network specialized for processing grid-like data such as images, which emerged as a powerful architecture for image recognition tasks. They utilize convolutional layers to automatically learn hierarchical representations of visual features, leading to state-of-the-art performance on image classification, object detection, and other computer vision tasks. The Recurrent Neural Networks (RNNs) are another class of neural networks designed to process sequences of data, making them well-suited for tasks such as language modeling, speech recognition, and time series prediction. They have been extended with variations such as Long Short-Term Memory (LSTM) and Gated Recurrent Unit (GRU) cells, which address the vanishing gradient problem and improve the ability of RNNs to learn long-range dependencies. With advances in deep learning research, the Transformer architecture, introduced in the paper "Attention is All You Need" by Vaswani et al. in 2017, has revolutionized the natural language processing (NLP) by introducing self-attention mechanisms that capture long-range dependencies in text data. Models like BERT (Bidirectional Encoder Representations from Transformers) and GPT (Generative Pre-trained Transformer) have achieved state-of-the-art results in various NLP tasks.

These milestones represent just a fraction of the rich history of artificial neural networks. The field continues to evolve rapidly, driven by advances in research, technology, and the increasing demand for AI-powered solutions in various domains. The ANN and its building blocks have been discussed in this chapter.

7.2 NEURONS

In ANNs, neurons are the basic computational units that process and transmit information. They are inspired by the neurons in the human brain, though the computational model simplifies many aspects of the biological neurons. Some but of the key points about neurons in neural networks are discussed below:

- **Inputs and Outputs:** Neurons in a neural network receive input signals from other neurons or directly from the input data. They process these inputs using a mathematical operation and produce an output signal, which is transmitted to other neurons in the network or serves as the final output of the network.

- **Activation Function:** Neurons typically apply an activation function to the weighted sum of their inputs before producing an output. This activation function introduces non-linearity into the network, allowing it to learn complex relationships in the data. Common activation functions include the sigmoid function, hyperbolic tangent (tanh) function, rectified linear unit (ReLU), variants like Leaky ReLU, etc.
- **Weights and Biases:** Each input to a neuron is associated with a weight, which determines its contribution to the neuron's output. Additionally, neurons usually have an associated bias term, which allows them to influence the output independent of the input. During training, the weights and biases of neurons are adjusted to minimize the difference between the predicted and actual outputs of the network.
- **Layers and Architectures:** Neurons are organized into layers within a neural network. The input layer receives input data, hidden layers process the data through intermediate computations, and the output layer produces the final output of the network. The arrangement of neurons into layers and the connections between them define the architecture of the neural network, which can vary widely depending on the task and complexity of the problem.
- **Learning:** Neurons in a neural network learn by adjusting their weights and biases based on feedback from the training data. This learning process, typically performed using algorithms such as backpropagation, enables the network to improve its performance over time by minimizing errors in its predictions.

Overall, neurons are the fundamental building blocks of neural networks, and their interactions through weighted connections enable the network to learn from data and perform complex computations, making them a powerful tool for machine learning and artificial intelligence applications. The Figure 7.1 explains the neuron and its components.

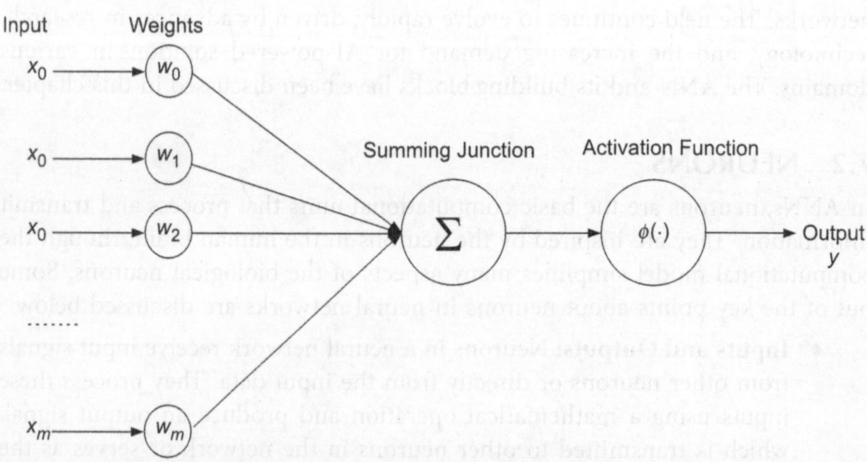

Figure 7.1 Neural networks neuron block diagram.

7.3 LAYERS

Neural networks consist of multiple layers, each serving a specific purpose in transforming input data into useful outputs. Neural networks include mainly three types of layers—input, hidden and output layers. Input Layer receives input data and passes it to the next layer. The number of nodes in this layer corresponds to the number of features in the input data. Hidden Layers are situated between the input and output layers. They perform computations on the input data through weighted connections and activation functions. Deep neural networks contain multiple hidden layers. Output Layer is the final layer in the network and produces the model's output. The number of nodes in this layer depends on the problem being solved. For example, in binary classification, there may be one node for each class with a sigmoid activation function. In multiclass classification, there might be one node per class with a softmax activation function.

The hidden layers could be of different nature like dense, convolutional, pooling, recurrent, Long Short-Term Memory (LSTM) and Gated Recurrent Unit (GRU) layers. Dense (Fully Connected) Layer is the one in which each node of the layer is connected to every node of the previous layer. These layers are common in traditional feedforward neural networks. In case of convolutional layer, Convolutional Neural Networks (CNNs) use convolutional layers to detect spatial patterns in images. Each neuron in a convolutional layer is connected to only a local region of the input volume, which helps in preserving spatial relationships.

Pooling layers are often used in conjunction with convolutional layers in CNNs. They reduce the spatial dimensions of the convolutional layers, which helps in decreasing computational complexity and controlling overfitting. In recurrent layer, Recurrent Neural Networks (RNNs) utilize recurrent layers to process sequences of data. These layers maintain internal state (hidden state) and take both the current input and the previous hidden state as input. The LSTM is a type of recurrent layer. LSTMs are designed to better capture long-term dependencies in sequential data. They have a more complex architecture compared to traditional recurrent layers, with mechanisms for selectively remembering or forgetting information. GRU Layer is similar to LSTM. GRU is another type of recurrent layer that also addresses the vanishing gradient problem. It has a simpler architecture compared to LSTM, with fewer parameters.

Each type of layer serves a specific function in the neural network architecture and the arrangement and combination of these layers vary depending on the task at hand and the complexity of the data being processed. A typical arrangement of input, hidden and output layers has been shown in Figure 7.2.

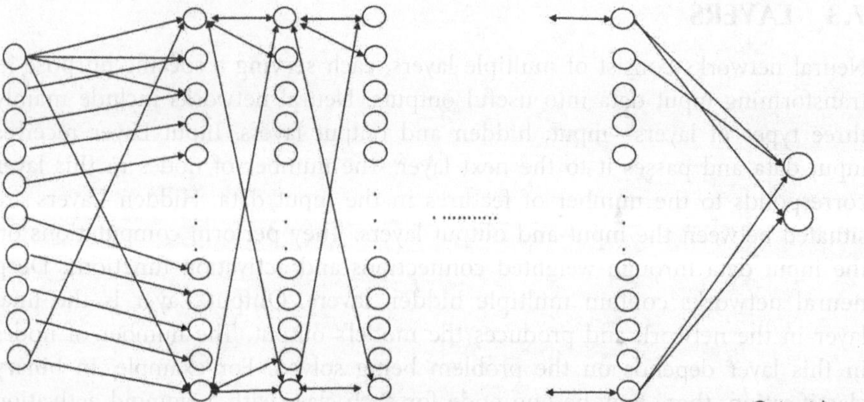

Figure 7.2 Input, hidden and output layers in neural networks.

7.4 ACTIVATION FUNCTION

Activation functions play a crucial role in neural networks by introducing non-linearity, enabling the network to learn complex patterns in data. Some of the commonly used activation functions are discussed below.

- **Sigmoid Function:** It is based on the formula $\sigma(x)=\frac{1}{1+e^{-x}}$ and output range is between 0 and 1. Smooth gradient is one of its property.
- **Hyperbolic Tangent (tanh):** It is based on the formula $\tanh(x)=\frac{e^x-e^{-x}}{e^x+e^{-x}}$ and output range is between –1 to 1.
- **Rectified Linear Unit (ReLU):** It is based on the formula ReLU(x) = max(0, x) and output range is between 0 and ∞. It is simple, computationally coefficient, and avoids vanishing gradient problem. However, it's not zero-centered, and it can suffer from the "dying ReLU" problem where neurons output zero for all inputs.
- **Leaky ReLU:** It is based on the formula Leaky ReLU(x) = max(αx, x), where α is a small constant (< 1) and output range is between –∞ and +∞. This function addresses the "dying ReLU" problem by allowing a small gradient when the input is negative.
- **Exponential Linear Unit (ELU):** It is based on the formula

  $$\text{ELU}(x)=\begin{cases} x & \text{if } x>0 \\ \alpha(e^x-1) & \text{if } x\le 0 \end{cases}$$

  Its output range is –∞ and ∞. It is similar to ReLU but with smoother gradients and negative values for negative inputs.
- **Softmax:** It is based on the formula $\text{Softmax}(x_i)=\frac{e^{x_i}}{\sum_{j=1}^{N} e^{x_j}}$ for i = 1, 2,

…, N. Its output range is between 0 and 1 for each neuron and sum of outputs equal to 1. This function is typically used in the output layer for multiclass classification, as it converts raw scores into probabilities.

These activation functions are applied element-wise to the output of each neuron in the network's hidden layers, introducing non-linearities that enable the network to learn complex relationships between input and output. The choice of activation function depends on the specific characteristics of the problem being solved and the network architecture.

7.5 WEIGHTS AND BIASES

In a neural network, weights play a crucial role in determining the output of the network given a set of inputs. Weights represent the strength of connections between neurons in different layers of the network. Each connection between neurons has an associated weight that controls the signal passing from one neuron to another. During the training process of a neural network, these weights are adjusted iteratively through a process called backpropagation, where the network learns from the input data and adjusts the weights to minimize the difference between the predicted output and the actual output. This adjustment of weights is what enables the network to learn and improve its performance on tasks such as classification or regression. Weights are initialized randomly at the beginning of the training process and are updated through optimization algorithms such as gradient descent or its variants. The values of these weights determine the behavior of the neural network, including its ability to generalize well to unseen data.

Bias terms are additional parameters that are added to each neuron's input before the activation function is applied. They allow neural networks to represent more complex functions and make them more flexible in modeling real-world data. Each neuron in a neural network typically has its own bias term, which is a constant value. When the network processes input data, the bias term is added to the weighted sum of the inputs before passing through the activation function. This bias essentially allows the activation function to be shifted left or right, influencing the output of the neuron. The role of the bias term is to provide the network with flexibility to learn and represent patterns in the data that might not be centered at the origin. Without bias terms, the neural network would only be able to learn functions that pass through the origin of the coordinate system, limiting its expressive power. During the training process of a neural network, the values of bias terms are also adjusted along with the weights through optimization algorithms such as gradient descent. This adjustment allows the network to learn the optimal bias values that minimize the difference between the predicted output and the actual output on the training data.

7.6 BACKPROPAGATION

Backpropagation is a fundamental algorithm for training neural networks. It's used to update the weights of the network's connections in order to minimize the difference between the predicted output and the actual output of the network. The common parts of backpropagation that happen in sequential order are explained below:

- **Forward Pass (Feed forward Propagation):** During the forward pass, input data is propagated through the neural network layer by layer, from the input layer to the output layer. Each neuron computes a weighted sum of its inputs, adds a bias term, and applies an activation function to produce an output. The output of each neuron becomes the input to the neurons in the next layer and this process continues until the output layer is reached.
- **Compute Loss:** Once the forward pass is complete the output of the neural network is compared to the actual output (ground truth) using a loss function. The loss function measures the discrepancy between the predicted output and the actual output of the network. Common loss functions include mean squared error for regression tasks and cross-entropy loss for classification tasks.
- **Backward Pass (Backpropagation):** Backpropagation involves computing the gradient of the loss function with respect to each weight and bias in the network. It starts from the output layer and moves backward through the network to compute the gradients layer by layer. The chain rule from calculus is used to compute these gradients efficiently.
- **Gradient Descent:** Once the gradients of the loss function with respect to the network parameters (weights and biases) are computed, the weights and biases are updated in the opposite direction of the gradient to minimize the loss function. This update is typically performed using an optimization algorithm, such as gradient descent, stochastic gradient descent (SGD), or Adam optimization.
- **Iterative Process:** The above four steps are repeated iteratively for multiple epochs or until a stopping criterion is met, such as reaching a certain level of accuracy or the loss function converging to a minimum.

Backpropagation allows the neural network to learn from its mistakes by adjusting its parameters (weights and biases) to improve its performance on a given task. It is a foundational algorithm in training neural networks and has enabled the development of deep learning models capable of solving complex real-world problems. The algorithm that follows above steps has been explained in Algorithm 10.

Algorithm 10 Backpropagation algorithm

Forward Computation:

$v_j^{(l)}(n) = \sum_{i=0}^{m_0} w_{ji}^{(l)}(n) y_i^{(l-1)}(n);$

$y_j^{(l)} = \phi_j(v_j(n))$

Backward Computation:

$\delta_j^{(l)}(n) = e_j^{(L)}(n)\phi_j'(v_j^L(n))$, for neuron j in output layer L;

$\delta_j^{(l)}(n) = f_j'(v_j^l n)) \sum_k \delta_k^{(l+1)}(n) w_{kj}^{(l+1)}(n)$

Weights updates in layer l:

$w_{ji}^{(l)}(n+1) = w_{ji}^{(l)}(n) + \alpha[w_{ji}^{(l)}(n-1)] + \eta\delta_j^{(l)}(n) y_i^{(l-1)}(n)$

In Algorithm 10, the working has been presented with an instance of one hidden layer to another consecutive hidden layer for neuron j to neuron k. The first step, forward computation results in the output $y_j^{(l)}$ for neuron j in layer l. The forward computation is performed in forward direction until the output layer neuron value is not computed. In backward computation, gradient value is computed for neuron j in hidden layer l. One forward and backward computation together completes one iteration and updates the weight for next iteration. The adjustment of the synaptic weights of network in layer l is computed. Here, w_{ji} is the weight from i to j; $v_j^{(l)}(n)$ is neuron j in layer l; $y_j^{(l)}$ is output of neuron j in layer l; $\delta_j^{(l)}(n)$ is gradient for neuron j in layer l; $e_j^{(L)}(n)$ is error signal at layer L for neuron j; ϕ_j' is differentiation of activation function; η and α are the learning rate and momentum constant, respectively. The working of Algorithm 10 can be understood using simple example with an input layer, two hidden layers and output layer as demonstrated in Figures 7.3 to 7.11. The working of diagrams from Figure 7.3 to 7.11 has been explained in respective captions.

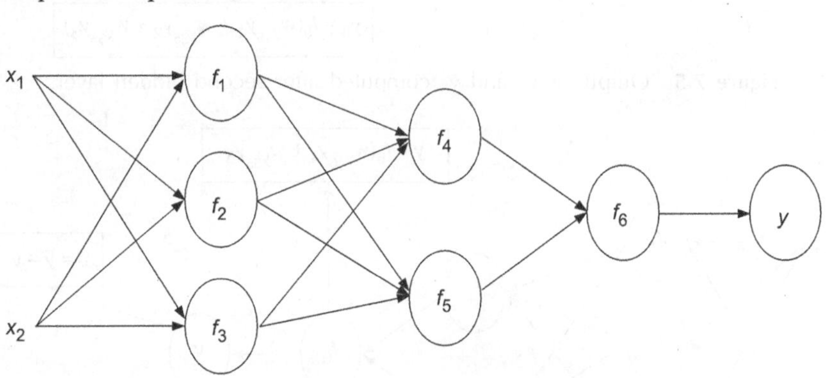

Figure 7.3 Neural networks initial setup with two hidden layers and two inputs as x_1 and x_2.

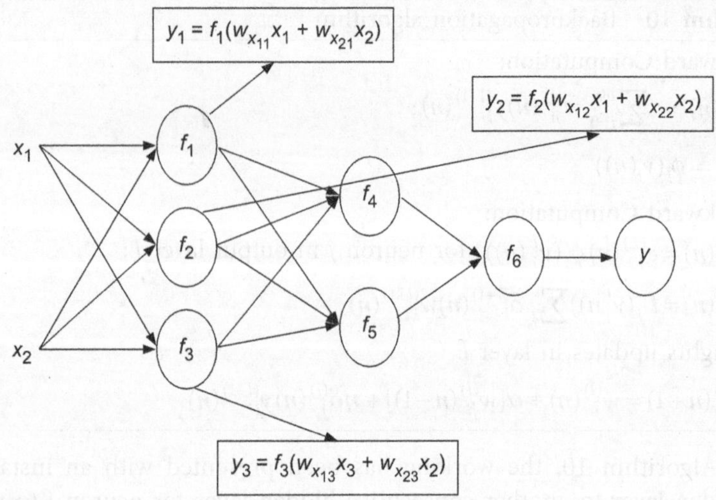

Figure 7.4 Output as y_1, y_2 and y_3 computed after first hidden layer.

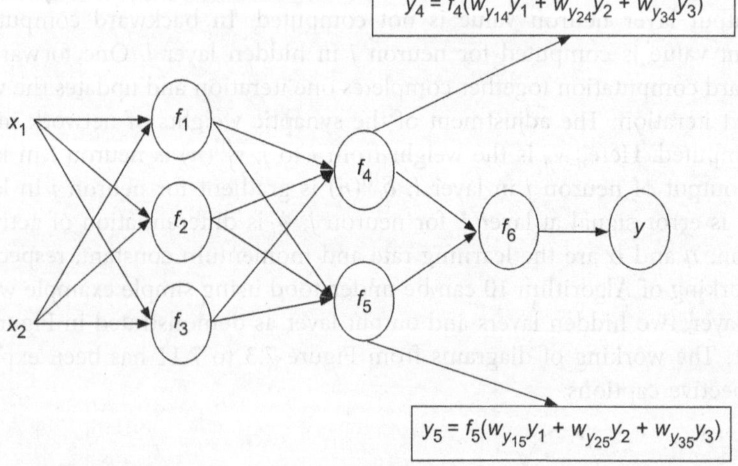

Figure 7.5 Output as y_4 and y_5 computed after second hidden layer.

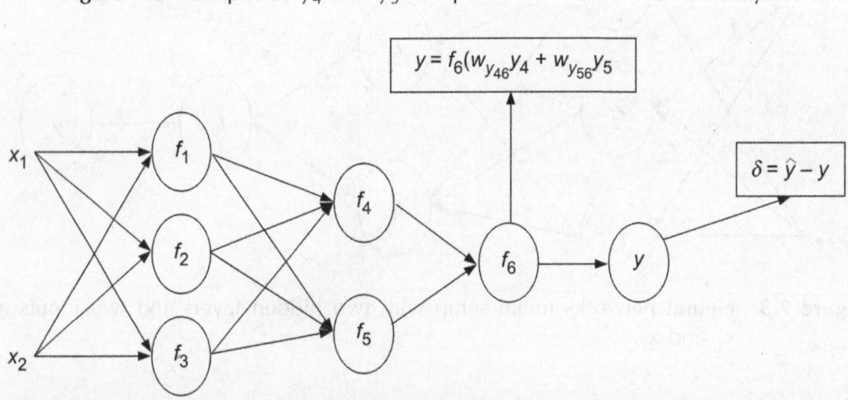

Figure 7.6 Output as y_6 and error δ computed after output layer.

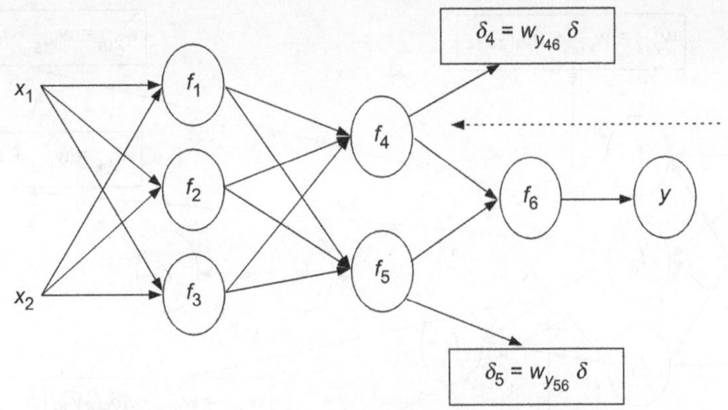

Figure 7.7 Backward computation step from output layer and respective δ_4 and δ_5 computed.

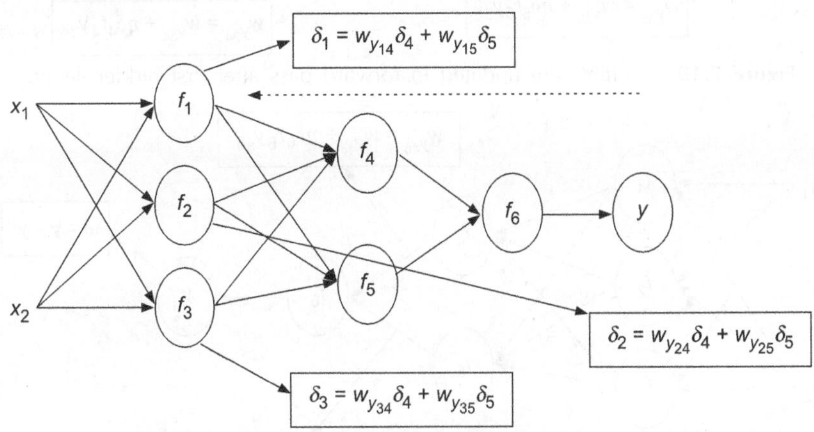

Figure 7.8 Backward computation and respective δ_1, δ_2 and δ_3 are computed.

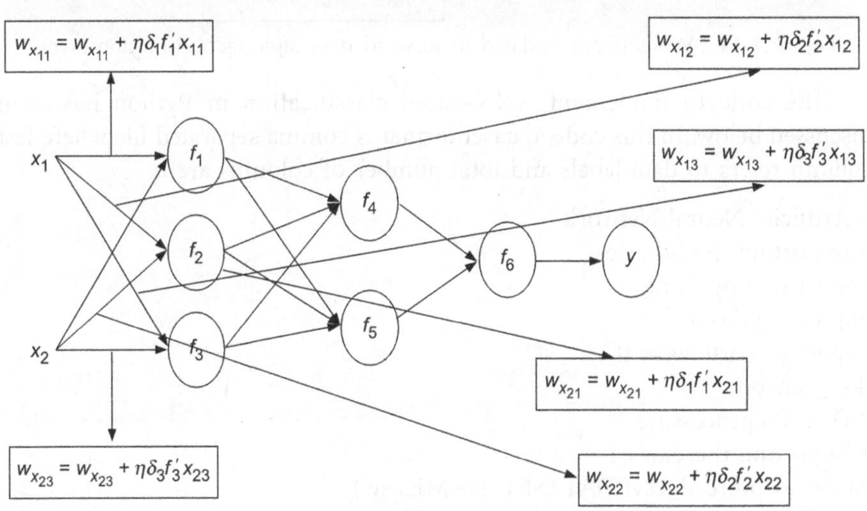

Figure 7.9 Weights are updated after first iteration including forward and backward pass.

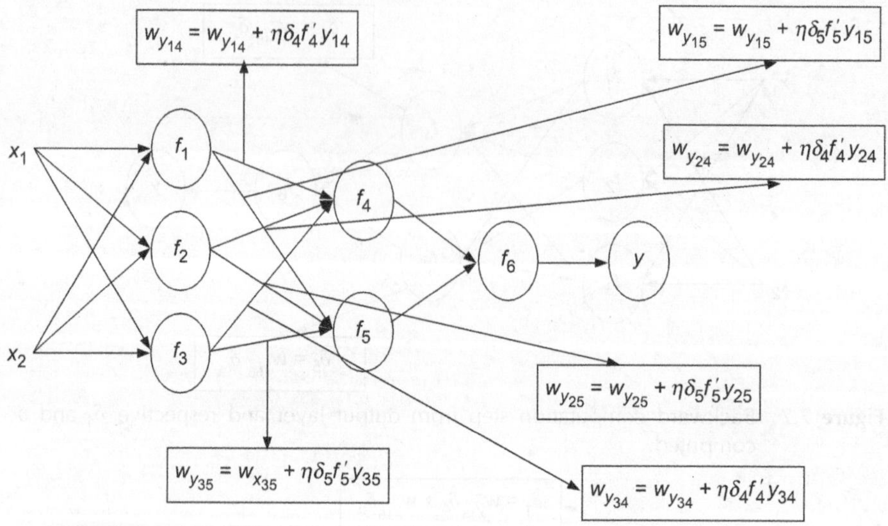

Figure 7.10 Weights are updated in forward pass after first hidden layer.

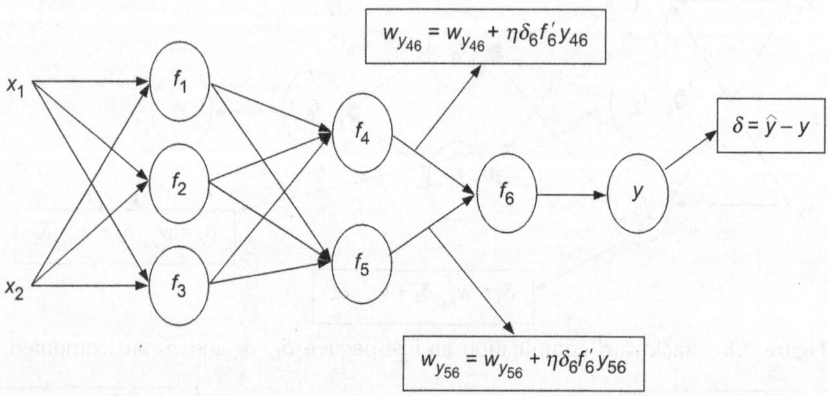

Figure 7.11 Weights are updated in forward pass after second hidden layer.

The code to implement ANN-based classification in Python has been discussed below. In this code, dataset format is comma separated file where last column refers to data labels and total number of columns are *n*.

```
# Artificial Neural Network
# Importing the libraries
import numpy as np
import pandas as pd
import tensorflow as tf
tf.__version__
# Data Preprocessing
# Importing the dataset
dataset = pd.read_csv('DATASET_NAME.csv')
X = dataset.iloc[:, :n].values
y = dataset.iloc[:, -1].values
```

```
# Feature Scaling
from sklearn.preprocessing import StandardScaler
sc = StandardScaler()
X = sc.fit_transform(X)
# Splitting the dataset into the Training set and Test set
from sklearn.model_selection import train_test_split
X_train, X_test, y_train, y_test = train_test_split(X, y, test_size = 0.2,
random_state = 0)

# Building the ANN
# Initializing the ANN
ann = tf.keras.models.Sequential()

# Adding the input layer and the first hidden layer
ann.add(tf.keras.layers.Dense(units=6, activation='relu'))

# Adding the second hidden layer
ann.add(tf.keras.layers.Dense(units=6, activation='relu'))

# Adding the output layer
ann.add(tf.keras.layers.Dense(units=1, activation='sigmoid'))

# Training the ANN
# Compiling the ANN
ann.compile(optimizer = 'adam', loss = 'binary_crossentropy', metrics =
['accuracy'])

# Training the ANN on the Training set
ann.fit(X_train, y_train, batch_size = 32, epochs = 100)
# Making the predictions and evaluating the model
# Predicting the Test set results
y_pred = ann.predict(X_test)
y_pred = (y_pred > 0.5)
print(np.concatenate((y_pred.reshape(len(y_pred),1),
y_test.reshape(len(y_test),1)),1))

# Making the Confusion Matrix
from sklearn.metrics import confusion_matrix
cm = confusion_matrix(y_test, y_pred)
print(cm)
```

7.7 UNSUPERVISED LEARNING USING NEURAL NETWORKS

Supervised and unsupervised learning are two fundamental approaches in machine learning. In supervised learning, the algorithm learns from labeled data, which means each input data point is associated with a corresponding target label. The goal of supervised learning is to learn a mapping from inputs to outputs based on the given labeled dataset, so that it can make predictions or decisions about unseen data. ANN is an example of supervised learning where label are required to train network. In unsupervised learning, the algorithm learns from unlabeled data, meaning there are no predefined target labels. The goal of unsupervised learning is to discover patterns, structures or relationships within the data. Clustering is a common task in unsupervised learning, where the algorithm groups similar data points together based on some similarity measure. The unsupervised learning could be implemented with neural networks as discussed in this chapter using self-organizing map. Both supervised and unsupervised learning have their own set of algorithms and techniques tailored to different types of data and tasks. Supervised learning is more common when labeled data is available, while unsupervised learning is useful for exploring and understanding the underlying structure of data when labeled data is scarce or unavailable.

7.8 SELF-ORGANIZING MAP

A Self-Organizing Map (SOM), also known as Kohonen map or Kohonen network, is a type of unsupervised learning neural network. It is used for dimensionality reduction and visualization of high-dimensional data, as well as for clustering and pattern recognition tasks. It mainly includes a network structure, weight initialization and updation using network training. A network structure is a SOM consisting of a grid of nodes, arranged in one or multiple dimensions (usually 2D or 3D). Each node is associated with a weight vector of the same dimensionality as the input data. The SOM initializes the weight vectors of the nodes with random values, often sampled from the input data. Training of SOM undergoes an iterative training process where it adjusts its weight vectors to better represent the input data. The training phase includes competition, cooperation and learning rate decay. In competition, for each input data point, the SOM finds the node whose weight vector is most similar to the input data point. This is typically done using a measure of distance, such as Euclidean distance. During cooperation, once the winning node (also known as the best matching unit) is determined, the neighboring nodes of the best matching unit also update their weight vectors to be closer to the input data point. The extent of this influence decreases with distance from the best matching unit. In learning rate decay, over time, the learning rate decreases, causing the rate of adjustment to slow down. This helps stabilize the convergence of the SOM.

The convergence of SOM happens after many iterations. The SOM converges to a stable state where the nodes are arranged in such a way that neighboring nodes represent similar input data points. This property makes

SOMs useful for clustering and visualizing high-dimensional data. The SOM algorithm has been discussed in Algorithm 11.

Algorithm 11 Self-Organizing Map algorithm

1. Initialize SOM grid with neurons as,
   (a) Create a grid of neurons, each associated with a weight vector.
   (b) Neurons are typically arranged in a 2D or 3D grid.
2. Initialize weights,
   (a) Randomly initialize the weight vectors for each neuron.
   (b) These weights can be sampled from the input data or from a random distribution.
3. Initialize learning rate (α), neighborhood radius (σ), and number of iterations (epochs).
4. Training loop,
   for epoch = 1 to N do
   (a) Randomly select an input vector from the dataset.
   (b) Find the best matching unit.
   (c) Update weights of best matching unit and its neighbors.
   (d) Update learning rate and neighborhood radius

end for

In Algorithm 11, a structure is designed where input layer includes input variables and output layer is the labels outcome. In step 2, weights are randomly assigned during initialization phase. The learning rate, neighborhood radius and number of iterations are initialized in step 3. In step 4, an input vector is randomly selected from dataset and its matching score evaluated between input vector and other weight vectors of grid. The best score is the best matching value. Euclidean distance is popular to compute similarity value. The weight vector of best matching unit is updated and its neighbouring neurons update learning rate and neighborhood radius. The step is applied for N number of times and value of N depends on the dataset sizes.

EXERCISES

7.1 How is artificial neural network is similar to biological neural network? Explain.

7.2 Discuss ANN components in detail.

7.3 What is a perceptron? How is it related to ANN?

7.4 What is multi-layer perceptron? Explain.

7.5 Discuss history of neural networks in brief.

7.6 Discuss neuron working with the help of a diagram.

7.7 Discuss four types of activation functions and display graphs of these activation functions.

7.8 Why weights and bias are important in neural networks?

7.9 How feedforward computation different from backward computation in neural networks?

7.10 What is role of forward computation in backpropagation? Explain.

7.11 Discuss importance of hidden layers.

7.12 Explain need of number of hidden layers in a neural network. How you decide how many hidden layers are required?

7.13 Discuss algorithm of backpropagation.

7.14 Discuss backpropagation working with help of diagram for 3 hidden layers and one iteration.

7.15 How ANN is an example of supervised learning? Explain.

7.16 Differentiate between supervised and unsupervised learning.

7.17 How unsupervised neural network works? Explain with examples.

7.18 Discuss algorithm of self-organizing map.

7.19 Implement SOM for the four input vectors as, $x = x_1, x_2, x_3, x_4$, where $x_1 = (1, 1, 0, 0)$, $x_2 = (0, 0, 0, 1)$, $x_3 = (1, 0, 0, 0)$ and $x_4 = (0, 0, 1, 1)$. Learning rate is $\alpha = 0.6$. Consider weights initialized for two output labels as, $\begin{bmatrix} 0.2 & 0.6 & 0.5 & 0.9 \\ 0.8 & 0.4 & 0.7 & 0.3 \end{bmatrix}$. Run algorithm for three iterations only.

CHAPTER 8

Classification Techniques

8.1 INTRODUCTION

Classification in machine learning is the process of categorizing data points into different classes or categories based on their features. It is a supervised learning task where the algorithm learns from labeled data to predict the class labels of new, unseen data points. The main objective of classification is to build a model that can accurately generalize from the training data to classify new instances correctly. This involves selecting appropriate features, choosing a suitable classification algorithm, training the model on labeled data and evaluating its performance using metrics like accuracy, precision, recall and F1-score. There are various classification algorithms, each with its own strengths and weaknesses. Common classifiers are listed below:

- **k-Nearest Neighbors:** A simple algorithm that classifies new data points based on the majority class of their k nearest neighbors in feature space.
- **Decision Trees:** A tree-like structure where each internal node represents a feature, each branch represents a decision based on that feature and each leaf node represents a class label.
- **Random Forest:** An ensemble learning method that builds multiple decision trees and combines their predictions to improve accuracy and reduce overfitting.
- **Support Vector Machines:** A powerful algorithm that finds the optimal hyperplane separating different classes in feature space.
- **Naive Bayes:** A probabilistic classifier based on Bayes' theorem, which assumes independence between features.
- **Logistic Regression:** A regression-based algorithm used for binary classification, which models the probability that a given input belongs to a particular class.
- **Neural Networks:** Deep learning models consisting of multiple layers of interconnected neurons, which can learn complex patterns from data.

The choice of algorithm depends on factors, such as the nature of the data, the size of the dataset, computational resources and the interpretability of the model. Classification is widely used in various real-world applications, including spam detection, sentiment analysis, image recognition, medical diagnosis, fraud detection and recommendation systems. The classifiers are discussed in detailed in the chapter.

8.2 *k*-NEAREST NEIGHBORS-BASED CLASSIFICATION

The *k*-Nearest Neighbors (*k*-NN) algorithm is a simple yet powerful non-parametric classification and regression technique. Classification with *k*-NN include two major steps:

- **Training Phase:** During training, the algorithm simply memorizes the entire training dataset.
- **Prediction Phase:** When predicting the class label of a new data point, the below given steps are followed:
  - Calculate the distance between the new data point and all the other points in the training set using a distance metric such as the Euclidean distance.
  - Identify the *k* nearest neighbors of the new data point based on the calculated distances.
  - Assign the class label to the new data point by majority voting among its *k* nearest neighbors. For example, if $k = 3$ and two neighbors belong to class A while one belongs to class B, the new data point will be assigned to class A.

Choice of *k* is very crucial in this technique. The value of *k* determines how many neighbors are considered when making predictions. It is a hyperparameter that needs to be chosen carefully. A smaller value of *k* leads to more complex decision boundaries and may result in overfitting, while a larger value of *k* can lead to smoother decision boundaries but may underfit the data. Further, the choice of distance metric (e.g., Euclidean distance, Manhattan distance etc.) can significantly impact the performance of the algorithm, especially in high-dimensional spaces. Feature scaling is essential because *k*-NN is sensitive to the scale of features. Features with larger scales can dominate the distance calculations. Overall, computational cost is the main drawback of *k*-NN during the prediction phase, as it requires calculating distances between the new data point and all points in the training set. Despite its simplicity, *k*-NN can be surprisingly effective, especially in cases where the decision boundary is highly irregular or when the dataset is small. However, it may not perform well on high-dimensional data or when the dataset is imbalanced. The Figure 8.1 shows an example with 3 vs. 2 neighbors for a data point.

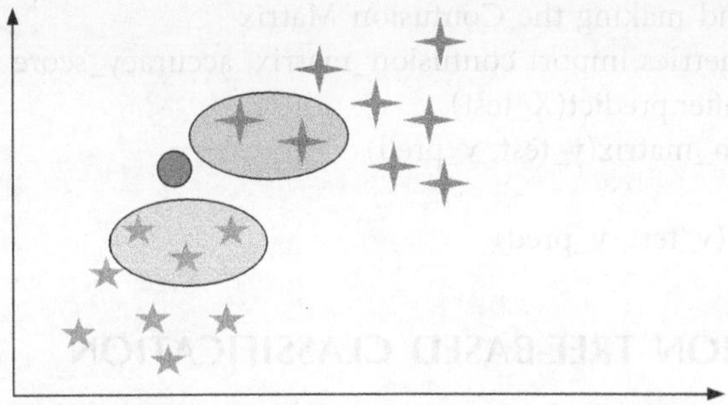

Figure 8.1 *k*-NN example with 3 vs. 2 neighbors.

The code to implement *k*-NN in Python has been discussed below. In this code, dataset is in csv format with *n* columns, where last column is data label and first *n* – 1 columns are features for respective data label.

```
#!/usr/bin/env python
# coding: utf-8
# K-Nearest Neighbors (K-NN)
# Importing the libraries
import numpy as np
import matplotlib.pyplot as plt
import pandas as pd

# Importing the dataset
dataset = pd.read_csv('DATASET_NAME.csv')
X = dataset.iloc[:, :n].values
y = dataset.iloc[:, -1].values

# Splitting the dataset into the Training set and Test set
from sklearn.model_selection import train_test_split
X_train, X_test, y_train, y_test = train_test_split(X, y, test_size = 0.25,
random_state = 0)

# Feature Scaling
from sklearn.preprocessing import StandardScaler
sc = StandardScaler()
X_train = sc.fit_transform(X_train)
X_test = sc.transform(X_test)

# Training the K-NN model on the Training set
from sklearn.neighbors import KNeighborsClassifier
classifier = KNeighborsClassifier(n_neighbors = 5, metric ='minkowski', p = 2)
classifier.fit(X_train, y_train)
```

```
# Prediction and making the Confusion Matrix
from sklearn.metrics import confusion_matrix, accuracy_score
y_pred = classifier.predict(X_test)
cm = confusion_matrix(y_test, y_pred)
print(cm)
accuracy_score(y_test, y_pred)
```

8.3 DECISION TREE-BASED CLASSIFICATION

A Decision Tree is a popular supervised learning algorithm used for both classification and regression tasks. It works by recursively partitioning the input space into regions, with each partition being associated with a specific class label or a predicted value. Working of decision tree includes two steps—tree construction and prediction. These steps are discussed below.

- **Tree Construction:**
  - At the root of the tree, choose the feature that best splits the data into subsets that are as pure as possible in terms of class labels. This process is typically based on metrics like Gini impurity or information gain.
  - Recursively repeat this process for each subset (or node) until one of the stopping criteria is met, such as reaching a maximum depth, reaching a minimum number of samples in a node or when further splitting does not improve purity.
- **Prediction:**
  - When making predictions for a new data point, traverse the decision tree from the root node to a leaf node based on the feature values of the data point.
  - The predicted class label is the majority class of the training samples in the leaf node.

The advantages of decision trees include—interpretability, handling non-linear relationships, no feature scaling and mixed data type handling. Interpretability in decision trees provide a clear and interpretable representation of the decision-making process. Handling nonlinear relationships in decision trees can capture nonlinear relationships between features and the target variable. Feature scaling is not required in decision trees as features are not sensitive to the scale of features. Handling mixed data types in decision trees can handle both numerical and categorical features without requiring feature encoding. However, decision trees also have some limitations, such as overfitting, instability, bias and less expressiveness. Overfitting in decision trees could happen easily, especially when they are allowed to grow too deep or when trained on noisy data. Instability are small changes in the data that can lead to significantly different trees, making decision trees unstable. Bias towards dominant classes happen in classification tasks with imbalanced class distributions, decision trees tend to favor the dominant classes. Limited Expressiveness in decision trees may not be able to capture complex relationships in the data as effectively as other algorithms like neural networks. To address some of these limitations, ensemble methods like random forests and gradient boosting machines are often used, which combine multiple decision trees to improve predictive performance and robustness. The code to implement decision tree classification in Python has been discussed below. In this code, dataset is in csv format with *n* columns, where last column is data label and first *n* – 1 columns are features for respective data label.

```
#!/usr/bin/env python
# coding: utf-8
# Decision Tree Classification

# Importing the libraries
import numpy as np
import matplotlib.pyplot as plt
import pandas as pd

# Importing the dataset
dataset = pd.read_csv('DATASET_NAME.csv')
X = dataset.iloc[:, :n].values
y = dataset.iloc[:, -1].values

# Splitting the dataset into the Training set and Test set
from sklearn.model_selection import train_test_split
X_train, X_test, y_train, y_test = train_test_split(X, y,
test_size = 0.25, random_state = 0)

# Feature Scaling
from sklearn.preprocessing import StandardScaler
sc = StandardScaler()
X_train = sc.fit_transform(X_train)
X_test = sc.transform(X_test)

# Training the Decision Tree Classification model on the
#Training set
from sklearn.tree import DecisionTreeClassifier
classifier = DecisionTreeClassifier(criterion = 'entropy', random_state = 0)
classifier.fit(X_train, y_train)

# Prediction and making the Confusion Matrix
from sklearn.metrics import confusion_matrix, accuracy_score
```

```
y_pred = classifier.predict(X_test)
cm = confusion_matrix(y_test, y_pred)
print(cm)
accuracy_score(y_test, y_pred)
```

8.4 RANDOM FOREST-BASED CLASSIFICATION

Random forest classification is a powerful machine learning algorithm used for both classification and regression tasks. Random forests or random decision forests is an ensemble learning method for classification, regression and other tasks that operates by constructing a multitude of decision trees at training time. For classification tasks, the output of the random forest is the class selected by most trees. The working of random forest technique includes four major steps—sampling, feature selection, decision tree construction and voting.

- **Random Sampling:** Random forest randomly selects a subset of data from the dataset (with replacement) to train each decision tree. This process is known as bootstrapping.
- **Random Feature Selection:** At each node of the decision tree, a random subset of features is considered for splitting. This helps in reducing correlation between trees and makes the model more robust.
- **Decision Tree Construction:** Each decision tree is constructed based on the randomly sampled data and features. The trees are typically grown to their maximum depth without pruning.
- **Voting:** During prediction, each tree in the forest independently predicts the class of the input data point. The final prediction is then determined by aggregating the votes from all the trees (for classification).

Random forest has several advantages, including its ability to handle large datasets with high dimensionality, its resistance to overfitting, and its capability to provide feature importance scores. It is widely used in various fields, such as finance, healthcare and marketing for tasks like customer churn prediction, disease diagnosis and stock price forecasting, among others. The code to implement random forest classification in Python has been discussed below. In this code, dataset is in csv format with n columns, where last column is data label and first $n - 1$ columns are features for respective data label.

```
#!/usr/bin/env python
# coding: utf-8
# Random Forest Classification
# Importing the libraries
import numpy as np
import matplotlib.pyplot as plt
import pandas as pd
```

```
# Importing the dataset
dataset = pd.read_csv('DATASET_NAME.csv')
X = dataset.iloc[:, :n].values
y = dataset.iloc[:, -1].values

# Splitting the dataset into the Training set and Test set
from sklearn.model_selection import train_test_split
X_train, X_test, y_train, y_test = train_test_split(X, y, test_size = 0.25,
random_state = 0)

# Feature Scaling
from sklearn.preprocessing import StandardScaler
sc = StandardScaler()
X_train = sc.fit_transform(X_train)
X_test = sc.transform(X_test)

# Training the Random Forest Classification model on the
#Training set
from sklearn.ensemble import RandomForestClassifier
classifier = RandomForestClassifier(n_estimators = 10,
criterion = 'entropy', random_state = 0) classifier.fit(X_train, y_train)

# Prediction and making the Confusion Matrix
from sklearn.metrics import confusion_matrix, accuracy_score
y_pred = classifier.predict(X_test)
cm = confusion_matrix(y_test, y_pred)
print(cm)
accuracy_score(y_test, y_pred)
```

8.5 SUPPORT VECTOR MACHINES

A Support Vector Machine (SVM) is a powerful supervised learning algorithm used for classification and regression tasks. Its primary objective is to find the optimal hyperplane in an N-dimensional space that distinctly separates data points belonging to different classes. Working of SVM include the following components.

- **Hyperplane:** In a two-dimensional space, a hyperplane is a line that separates data points belonging to different classes. In higher dimensions, it is a subspace.
- **Support Vectors:** These are the data points closest to the hyperplane and have a crucial role in defining it. These points are essentially the ones that are most difficult to classify.

- **Margin:** The distance between the hyperplane and the support vectors is known as the margin. SVM aims to maximize this margin, as it signifies a clearer separation between classes and improves the model's generalization ability.
- **Kernel Trick:** SVM can efficiently handle non-linear data by transforming the input space into a higher-dimensional space using a kernel function. This allows it to find a hyperplane that separates classes even if they're not linearly separable in the original space.
- **C parameter:** This parameter controls the trade-off between maximizing the margin and minimizing the classification error. A smaller C value encourages a wider margin, potentially allowing more misclassifications, while a larger C value penalizes misclassifications more heavily, resulting in a narrower margin.

SVM can be implemented in primal or dual form. The popular way of using SVM is in dual form as data feature size is usually very large and dual form is more suitable to handle such data.

SVMs have several advantages, such as effective performance in high-dimensional spaces, robustness against overfitting (especially in high-dimensional spaces) and versatility in handling different types of data through the kernel trick. However, they can be sensitive to the choice of the kernel and the regularization parameter. The code to implement SVM classification in Python has been discussed below. In this code, dataset is in csv format with n columns, where last column is data label and first $n - 1$ columns are features for respective data label.

```
#!/usr/bin/env python
# coding: utf-8
# Support Vector Machine (SVM)
# Importing the libraries
import numpy as np
import matplotlib.pyplot as plt
import pandas as pd

# Importing the dataset
dataset = pd.read_csv('DATASET_NAME.csv')
X = dataset.iloc[:, :n].values
y = dataset.iloc[:, -1].values

# Splitting the dataset into the Training set and Test set
from sklearn.model_selection import train_test_split
X_train, X_test, y_train, y_test = train_test_split(X, y, test_size = 0.25,
random_state = 0)
```

```
# Feature Scaling
from sklearn.preprocessing import StandardScaler
sc = StandardScaler()
X_train = sc.fit_transform(X_train)
X_test = sc.transform(X_test)

# Training the SVM model on the Training set
from sklearn.svm import SVC
classifier = SVC(kernel = 'linear', random_state = 0)
classifier.fit(X_train, y_train)

# Prediction and making the Confusion Matrix
from sklearn.metrics import confusion_matrix, accuracy_score
y_pred = classifier.predict(X_test)
cm = confusion_matrix(y_test, y_pred)
print(cm)
accuracy_score(y_test, y_pred)
```

8.6 NAIVE BAYES CLASSIFICATION

Naive Bayes classification is a popular machine learning technique used for classification tasks. It is based on Bayes' theorem, which describes the probability of an event based on prior knowledge of conditions that might be related to the event.

In Naive Bayes classification, the "naive" assumption is that features are independent of each other, given the class label. Even though this assumption is often not true in real-world scenarios, Naive Bayes classifiers can still perform well and are particularly efficient and easy to implement. The common components of Naive Bayes are discussed below.

- **Bayes' Theorem:**

$$P(Y \mid X) = \frac{P(X \mid Y) \times P(Y)}{P(X)}$$

  where, $P(Y|X)$ is the probability of class Y given the input X. $P(X|Y)$ is the probability of observing input X given that the class is Y. $P(Y)$ is the prior probability of class Y. $P(X)$ is the prior probability of observing input X.

- **Naive Assumption:** Naive Bayes classifiers assume that all features are independent of each other given the class label. This simplifies the calculation of $P(X|Y)$.

- **Classification:** Given a new input instance X, the classifier calculates the probability of each class label Y based on Bayes' theorem. The class label with the highest probability is assigned to the input instance.

- **Naive Bayes Classifiers:** Gaussian Naive Bayes assumes that continuous features follow a Gaussian distribution. Multinomial Naive Bayes are suitable for classification with discrete features (e.g., word counts). Bernoulli Naive Bayes assumes binary features (e.g., presence or absence of a feature).
- **Training:** Estimate the prior probabilities $P(Y)$ and the conditional probabilities $P(X|Y)$ from the training data.
- **Prediction:** For a new instance X, calculate the probabilities of each class label Y using the trained model and select the class label with the highest probability.

Naive Bayes classifiers are commonly used in text classification tasks (like spam detection or sentiment analysis) and in situations where the independence assumption approximately holds true. They are particularly useful when dealing with large datasets and high-dimensional feature spaces. However, they may not perform well if the independence assumption is violated or if there's insufficient training data. The code to implement Naive Bayes classification in Python has been discussed below. In this code, dataset is in csv format with n columns, where last column is data label and first n – 1 columns are features for respective data label.

```
# Naive Bayes
# Importing the libraries
import numpy as np
import matplotlib.pyplot as plt
import pandas as pd

# Importing the dataset
dataset = pd.read_csv('DATASET_NAME.csv')
X = dataset.iloc[:, :n].values
y = dataset.iloc[:, -1].values

# Splitting the dataset into the Training set and Test set
from sklearn.model_selection import train_test_split
X_train, X_test, y_train, y_test = train_test_split(X, y, test_size = 0.25,
random_state = 0)

# Feature Scaling
from sklearn.preprocessing import StandardScaler
sc = StandardScaler()
X_train = sc.fit_transform(X_train)
X_test = sc.transform(X_test)
```

```
# Training the Naive Bayes model on the Training set
from sklearn.naive_bayes import GaussianNB
classifier = GaussianNB()
classifier.fit(X_train, y_train)

# Prediction and making the Confusion Matrix
from sklearn.metrics import confusion_matrix, accuracy_score
y_pred = classifier.predict(X_test)
cm = confusion_matrix(y_test, y_pred)
print(cm)
accuracy_score(y_test, y_pred)
```

8.7 LOGISTIC REGRESSION

Logistic Regression is another popular machine learning algorithm used for classification tasks. Despite its name, logistic regression is used for binary classification problems, where the target variable (the variable you're trying to predict) has only two possible outcomes. The common steps in logistic regression-based classification are discussed below:

- **Model Representation:** Logistic regression models the probability that a given input instance belongs to a particular class. It uses the logistic function (also called the Sigmoid function) to map the input features to a probability value between 0 and 1.

$$P(y=1|x;\theta)=\frac{1}{1+e^{-\theta^T x}}$$

$$P(y=0|x;\theta)=1-P(y=1|x;\theta)$$

  Here, x represents the input features, θ represents the parameters of the model and y represents the class label (1 or 0).

- **Decision Boundary:** The decision boundary is the line (or hyperplane) that separates the classes. In logistic regression, the decision boundary is linear, which means it is a straight line (or plane) in the feature space.
- **Training:** During training, logistic regression learns the optimal parameters θ that minimize the error between the predicted probabilities and the actual class labels. This is typically done using optimization algorithms like gradient descent.
- **Cost Function:** The cost function (also called the loss function) measures the difference between the predicted probabilities and the actual class labels. In logistic regression, the most commonly used cost function is the logistic loss (or cross-entropy loss).

$$J(\theta)=-\frac{1}{m}\sum_{i=1}^{m}[y^{(i)}\log(h_\theta(x^{(i)}))+(1-y^{(i)})\log(1-h_\theta(x^{(i)}))]$$

Here, m is the number of training examples, $h_{\theta(x)}$ is the predicted probability such that $y = 1$ given input x and y is the actual class label.

- **Regularization:** To prevent overfitting, regularization techniques like L1 regularization (Lasso) or L2 regularization (Ridge) can be added to the cost function.
- **Prediction:** After training, logistic regression predicts the probability that a new input instance belongs to the positive class (class 1) using the learned parameters θ. If the predicted probability is greater than a threshold (usually 0.5), the instance is classified as belonging to the positive class; otherwise, it is classified as belonging to the negative class.

Logistic regression is widely used in various fields, including healthcare (for disease prediction), marketing (for customer churn prediction), and finance (for credit risk assessment), among others. It is an interpretable algorithm and can be easily implemented. However, it assumes a linear relationship between the features and the log-odds of the target variable, which may not always hold true in practice. The code to implement Logistic regression-based classification in Python has been discussed below. In this code, dataset is in csv format with n columns, where last column is data label and first $n - 1$ columns are features for respective data label.

```
# Logistic Regression

# Importing the libraries
import numpy as np
import matplotlib.pyplot as plt
import pandas as pd

# Importing the dataset
dataset = pd.read_csv('DATASET_NAME.csv')
X = dataset.iloc[:, :n].values
y = dataset.iloc[:, -1].values

# Splitting the dataset into the Training set and Test set
from sklearn.model_selection import train_test_split
X_train, X_test, y_train, y_test = train_test_split(X, y, test_size = 0.25,
random_state = 0)

# Feature Scaling
from sklearn.preprocessing import StandardScaler
sc = StandardScaler()
X_train = sc.fit_transform(X_train)
X_test = sc.transform(X_test)
```

```
# Training the Logistic Regression model on the Training set
from sklearn.linear_model import LogisticRegression
classifier = LogisticRegression(random_state = 0)
classifier.fit(X_train, y_train)

# Making the Confusion Matrix
from sklearn.metrics import confusion_matrix, accuracy_score
y_pred = classifier.predict(X_test)
cm = confusion_matrix(y_test, y_pred)
print(cm)
accuracy_score(y_test, y_pred)
```

EXERCISES

8.1 What is classification and how is it different from regression?

8.2 List the classification techniques and their brief description.

8.3 Discuss the working of k-nearest neighbor classification.

8.4 Write a program to implement k-nearest neighbor classification. Display training and testing data plots.

8.5 Discuss the working of decision tree classification.

8.6 Write a program to implement decision tree classification. Display training and testing data plots.

8.7 Discuss the working of random forest classification.

8.8 Write a program to implement random forest classification. Display training and testing data plots.

8.9 Discuss the working of support vector machine classification.

8.10 Write a program to implement support vector machine classification. Display training and testing data plots.

8.11 Discuss the working of Naive Bayes classification.

8.12 Write a program to implement Naive Bayes classification. Display training and testing data plots.

8.13 Discuss the working of logistic regression as a classification technique.

8.14 Write a program to implement logistic regression for classification. Display training and testing data plots.

8.15 Discuss the role of loss function in classifier.

8.16 How is SVM a convex problem? Explain.

8.17 Differentiate between linear and non-linear SVM.

8.18 Explain decision tree with the help of small data example.

8.19 How random forest depends on decision tree? Explain.

8.20 Does neural network work as a classifier? Explain.

CHAPTER 9

Clustering Techniques

Clustering is a type of unsupervised learning technique used to group similar data points together based on their characteristics or features. The goal of clustering is to partition a dataset into subsets, or clusters, such that, data points within the same cluster are more similar to each other than to those in other clusters. Data representation is the first task in clustering. Clustering algorithms operate on a dataset represented by a matrix, where rows correspond to data points (instances) and columns correspond to features. Each data point is described by its feature values. The other common component is distance metric. Clustering algorithms measure similarity or dissimilarity between data points using a distance metric. Common distance metrics include Euclidean distance, Manhattan distance, cosine similarity and others. The choice of distance metric depends on the nature of the data and the clustering algorithm being used. Cluster alignment required during the clustering process. The clustering algorithms assign data points to clusters iteratively based on their similarity. Initially, each data point may be assigned to its own cluster or randomly assigned to existing clusters. The algorithm then iteratively updates cluster assignments to minimize a predefined objective function, such as minimizing the intra-cluster distance or maximizing inter-cluster distance. Further, cluster centroids are computed to form cluster boundary. Some clustering algorithms like K-means, use cluster centroids as representatives of the cluster. They are computed as the mean or median of feature values of data points within the cluster.

The different types of clustering algorithms are *K*-means, hierarchical clustering, density-based clustering, and Gaussian mixture models. The evaluation of clustering algorithm is challenging since it is an unsupervised task. Common evaluation metrics include silhouette score, Davies–Bouldin index and others, which measure the compactness and separation of clusters. The clustering applications are used in various fields, such as customer segmentation, image segmentation, anomaly detection and recommendation systems. Clustering is an essential tool in exploratory data analysis and pattern recognition. Choosing the right clustering algorithm and parameters depends on the data characteristics, the desired number of clusters, and the specific problem domain.

9.1 *K*-MEANS CLUSTERING

K-means clustering is a popular unsupervised machine learning algorithm used for clustering similar data points into groups or clusters. The goal of *k*-means is to partition a dataset into *k* clusters, where each data point belongs to the cluster with the nearest mean (center). The steps involved in *k*-means algorithm are:

- **Initialization:** Choose *k* initial centroids randomly from the dataset. These centroids represent the centers of the clusters.
- **Assignment:** Assign each data point to the nearest centroid, forming *k* clusters.
- **Update:** Recalculate the centroids of the clusters by taking the mean of all data points assigned to each cluster.
- **Repeat:** Repeat steps 2 and 3 until the centroids no longer change significantly or the specified number of iteration is reached.

The algorithm converges when the centroids stabilize, i.e., when the clusters no longer change. However, it may converge to a local minimum, so it's common to run *k*-means multiple times with different initial centroids and choose the solution with the lowest total within-cluster variation (sum of squared distances from each point to its cluster centroid). *K*-means has several applications, including customer segmentation, image compression, anomaly detection, and more. However, it's worth noting that k-means can struggle with clusters of varying sizes, densities, and non-linear shapes.

In the *k*-means algorithm, the number of clusters, denoted as *k*, is typically specified by the user before running the algorithm. The algorithm then partitions the data into *k* clusters based on this predetermined number. Selecting the appropriate number of clusters (*k*) is an essential step in applying k-means effectively. However, determining the optimal *k* value can be challenging and often involves some trial and error or more sophisticated techniques. Elbow method, silhouette score, gap statistics and cross-validation are a few common methods to find the optimal value of *k*.

- **Elbow Method:** The elbow method involves running *k*-means for a range of *k* values and plotting the sum of squared distances (inertia) of data points to their assigned centroids for each *k*. The point where the inertia starts to decrease at a slower rate (forming an "elbow" in the plot) can be a good indication of the optimal *k* value.
- **Silhouette Score:** Silhouette score measures how similar an object is to its own cluster (cohesion) compared to other clusters (separation). It ranges from –1 to 1, where a high value indicates that the object is well matched to its own cluster and poorly matched to neighboring clusters. The optimal *k* value is often associated with the highest silhouette score.

- **Gap Statistics:** Gap statistics compare the inertia of the clustering algorithm on the actual data with the expected inertia obtained from a reference distribution (e.g., random data). The optimal *k* value is the one that maximizes the gap between the actual and expected inertias.
- **Cross-Validation:** Splitting the data into training and validation sets and evaluating the performance of the *k*-means algorithm with different *k* values using a metric such as the silhouette score or within-cluster sum of squares.

These methods provide guidelines for selecting the optimal number of clusters, but ultimately, the choice of *k* may also depend on domain knowledge and the specific goals of the analysis.

9.2 HIERARCHICAL CLUSTERING

Hierarchical clustering is an unsupervised machine learning way for clustering similar data points. Unlike k-means, which partitions the data into a pre-specified number of clusters, hierarchical clustering builds a hierarchy of clusters. There are two main types of hierarchical clustering:

- **Agglomerative Hierarchical Clustering:** This is a "bottom-up" approach where each data point starts as its own cluster and, at each step, the two closest clusters are merged until only one cluster remains. The result is a dendrogram that shows the hierarchical relationship between clusters.
- **Divisive Hierarchical Clustering:** This is a "top-down" approach where all data points start in one cluster, and at each step, the cluster that maximizes dissimilarity within clusters is split until each data point is in its own cluster. This approach is less common in practice due to its computational complexity.

For common understanding, process of agglomerative hierarchical clustering include following steps:

- **Initialization:** Start with each data point as its own cluster.
- **Compute Distance:** Compute the distance (similarity) between each pair of clusters. The choice of distance metric (e.g., Euclidean distance, Manhattan distance, etc.) depends on the nature of the data.
- **Merge Closest Clusters:** Merge the two closest clusters into a single cluster. The distance between clusters can be based on single linkage (minimum distance), complete linkage (maximum distance), average linkage, or other linkage criteria.
- **Update Distance Matrix:** Recalculate the distances between the new cluster and all other clusters.
- **Repeat:** Repeat steps 2-4 until all data points are in a single cluster or until a stopping criterion is met.

One advantage of hierarchical clustering is that it doesn't require specifying the number of clusters beforehand, and the dendrogram provides a visual representation of the clustering process, allowing users to interpret the hierarchy at different levels of granularity. However, hierarchical clustering can be computationally expensive, especially for large datasets, and the choice of distance metric and linkage criterion can significantly impact the results.

9.3 DENSITY-BASED CLUSTERING

Density-based clustering is a method for discovering clusters in data sets with arbitrary shapes and sizes. Unlike partition-based clustering algorithms like k-means, density-based clustering algorithms do not require the number of clusters to be specified in advance and can handle noise effectively. One of the most popular density-based clustering algorithms is DBSCAN (Density-Based Spatial Clustering of Applications with Noise). The working of density-based clustering includes the following steps:

- **Density Reachability:** DBSCAN defines clusters as dense regions of data points separated by regions of lower density. It starts by selecting a random point from the dataset. Then it identifies all the points in its "neighborhood" within a specified distance *r*.
- **Core Points:** If the number of points in the neighborhood exceeds a certain threshold (MinPts), the selected point is labeled as a "core point". Core points are indicative of regions of high density.
- **Density Connectivity:** DBSCAN then expands clusters by recursively adding neighboring core points to the cluster. A point is considered part of a cluster if it is a core point or is "density-reachable" from a core point.
- **Border Points and Noise:** Points that are not core points but are reachable from a core point (i.e., they lie within the *r*-neighborhood of a core point) are labeled as "border points". Points that are neither core points nor reachable from a core point are labeled as noise.

DBSCAN has several advantages, including its ability to handle clusters of arbitrary shapes and sizes, its robustness to noise, and its ability to discover the number of clusters automatically. However, it also has some limitations, such as its sensitivity to the choice of *r* and MinPts parameters and its performance degradation in high-dimensional spaces.

9.4 GAUSSIAN MIXTURE MODEL CLUSTERING

Gaussian Mixture Model (GMM) clustering is a probabilistic model that represents the distribution of data as a mixture of multiple Gaussian distributions. Unlike density-based clustering algorithms, GMM assumes that the data is generated from a mixture of several Gaussian distributions with unknown parameters. The working of GMM working includes the following steps:

- **Initialization:** GMM starts by randomly initializing the parameters of the Gaussian distributions that represent the clusters. These parameters include the mean, covariance matrix, and mixing coefficients (weights) for each Gaussian component.
- **Expectation-Maximization (EM) Algorithm:** GMM employs the EM algorithm to iteratively update the parameters to maximize the likelihood of the observed data. The EM algorithm consists of two main steps:
- **Expectation (E-step):** In this step, for each data point, GMM calculates the probability that it belongs to each Gaussian component based on the current parameters.
- **Maximization (M-step):** In this step, GMM updates the parameters of each Gaussian component based on the weighted sum of the data points, where the weights are the probabilities calculated in the E-step.
- **Convergence:** GMM iterates between the E-step and M-step until the algorithm converges, meaning that the parameters stabilize and do not change significantly between iterations, or until a predefined convergence criterion is met.
- **Cluster Assignment:** Once the parameters have converged, GMM assigns each data point to the Gaussian component with the highest probability.

The GMM clustering has several advantages, including its ability to model complex data distributions with multiple clusters that may have overlapping regions. It is also capable of estimating the uncertainty associated with each data point's assignment to a cluster through the probabilities computed during the E-step. However, GMM is sensitive to the initialization of parameters, and it may converge to local optima depending on the initialization strategy. Additionally, GMM assumes that the data within each cluster follows a Gaussian distribution, which may not always be appropriate for all data sets.

EXERCISES

9.1 What is clustering? Write a short note on advantages of clustering in data science.

9.2 How unsupervised learning can be implemented using clustering?

9.3 Write a short note on different types of clustering.

9.4 Discuss the working of *k*-means clustering working.

9.5 Write a program for the implementation of *k*-means clustering.

9.6 How can the optimal value of *k* be evaluated in *k*-means clustering?

9.7 Discuss hierarchical clustering in detail.

9.8 Compare *k*-means vs hierarchical clustering.

9.9 What is density-based clustering? Discuss its working.

9.10 How is DBSCAN important in data clustering? Explain.

9.11 Discuss GMM clustering.

9.12 Discuss the working steps of Guassian mixture model clustering technique.

9.13 Implement *k*-means, heirarchical, density based and GMM clustering through programming.

CHAPTER 10

Dimension Reduction Techniques

Dimensionality reduction techniques are methods used to reduce the number of input variables or features in a dataset while preserving the most important information. These techniques are particularly useful in machine learning and data analysis for various reasons, including mitigating the curse of dimensionality, reducing computational complexity, and facilitating visualization. Common dimensionality reduction techniques are principal component analysis, linear discriminant analysis, t-Distributed stochastic neighbor embedding, autoencoders, isometric mapping, and locally linear embedding. Principal Component Analysis (PCA) is one of the most widely used techniques for dimensionality reduction. It transforms the original variables into a new set of uncorrelated variables called principal components. Principal components are ordered in such a way that the first few capture the maximum variance in the data. The PCA finds linear combinations of the original variables that maximize variance. Linear Discriminant Analysis (LDA) is a supervised dimensionality reduction technique that aims to find the feature subspace that maximizes class separability. It projects the data onto a lower-dimensional space while preserving class discriminatory information. LDA aims to maximize the between-class scatter and minimize the within-class scatter. t-Distributed Stochastic Neighbor Embedding (t-SNE) is a nonlinear dimensionality reduction technique commonly used for visualization. It aims to preserve the local structure of the data points in the lower-dimensional space. t-SNE works well for visualizing high-dimensional data in two or three dimensions. Autoencoders are neural network architectures used for unsupervised learning of efficient data codings. They consist of an encoder network that maps the input data to a lower-dimensional latent space and a decoder network that reconstructs the input data from the latent space representation.Thus, by training the autoencoder to minimize the reconstruction error, the latent space captures the most important features of the data. Isomap (Isometric Mapping) is a nonlinear dimensionality reduction technique that aims to preserve the intrinsic geometry of the data.

It constructs a low-dimensional embedding of the data by preserving pairwise distances between data points. Isomap uses geodesic distances (shortest path distances) to capture the underlying manifold structure of the data. Locally Linear Embedding (LLE) is a nonlinear dimensionality reduction technique that preserves the local relationships between data points. It reconstructs each data point as a linear combination of its neighbors in the high-dimensional space. LLE seeks a low-dimensional representation where these local relationships are approximately preserved.

These techniques offer different approaches to reducing dimensionality, each with its own strengths and weaknesses. The choice of technique depends on factors, such as the nature of the data, the desired level of interpretability, and the specific goals of the analysis. In this chapter, we have only discussed PCA and LDA as dimension reduction techniques.

10.1 PRINCIPAL COMPONENT ANALYSIS

Principal Component Analysis (PCA) is a dimensionality reduction technique used to simplify the complexity in high-dimensional data while retaining trends and patterns. It works by transforming the original features of the data into a new set of orthogonal (uncorrelated) features called principal components. These components are ordered by the amount of variance they explain, with the first principal component explaining the most variance, the second explaining the second most, and so on. The working of PCA steps has been discussed below:

- **Standardization:** If the features have different scales, they are often standardized to have a mean of 0 and a standard deviation of 1.
- **Covariance Matrix Computation:** PCA computes the covariance matrix of the standardized data. The covariance between two variables measures how they vary together.
- **Eigenvalue Decomposition:** The PCA then performs eigenvalue decomposition or singular value decomposition on the covariance matrix. This yields eigenvectors and eigenvalues.
- **Selection of Principal Components:** The eigenvectors corresponding to the highest eigenvalues (explained variance) represent the principal components. Usually, only a subset of these components, which explain most of the variance, are retained.
- **Projection:** Finally, the original data are projected onto the subspace formed by the selected principal components.

The PCA is widely used in various fields such as image processing, finance, neuroscience, and many others to reduce the dimensionality of data while preserving important information. It helps in visualization, noise reduction, and speeding up learning algorithms by reducing the number of features. The code in python for PCA has been listed below. In this code, dataset is in csv format with n columns, where last column is data label and first $n-1$ columns are features for respective data label.

```
# Principal Component Analysis (PCA)

# Importing the libraries
import numpy as np
import matplotlib.pyplot as plt
import pandas as pd

# Importing the dataset
dataset = pd.read_csv('DATASET_NAME.csv')
X = dataset.iloc[:, :n].values
y = dataset.iloc[:, -1].values

# Feature Scaling
from sklearn.preprocessing import StandardScaler
sc = StandardScaler()
X = sc.fit_transform(X)

# Splitting the dataset into the Training set and Test set
from sklearn.model_selection import train_test_split
X_train, X_test, y_train, y_test = train_test_split(X, y, test_size = 0.2,
random_state = 0)

# Applying PCA
from sklearn.decomposition import PCA
pca = PCA(n_components = 2)
X_train = pca.fit_transform(X_train)
X_test = pca.transform(X_test)
explained_variance = pca.explained_variance_ratio_
```

10.2 LINEAR DISCRIMINANT ANALYSIS

Linear Discriminant Analysis (LDA) is a supervised dimensionality reduction technique used for classification tasks. Unlike PCA, which focuses on maximizing variance, LDA aims to maximize the separability between different classes in the data. The working of LDA is as follows:

- **Standardization:** Similar to PCA, if the features have different scales, they are often standardized to have a mean of 0 and a standard deviation of 1.
- **Between-Class and Within-Class Scatter Matrices:** LDA computes two matrices as Between-class scatter matrix which measures the scatter

between different classes in the data and Within-class scatter matrix which measures the scatter within each class.

- **Eigenvalue Decomposition:** LDA then performs eigenvalue decomposition on the matrix (Between-class scatter matrix)/(Within-class scatter matrix). This yields eigenvectors and eigenvalues.
- **Selection of Discriminant Directions:** The eigenvectors corresponding to the highest eigenvalues represent the directions (discriminants) that maximize the separation between classes.
- **Projection:** Finally, the original data are projected onto the subspace formed by the selected discriminant directions.

LDA is particularly useful when there are multiple classes in the data and the goal is to find a low-dimensional representation that maximizes class separability. It's commonly used in areas like face recognition, bioinformatics, and finance for feature extraction and dimensionality reduction before applying classification algorithms. The code in python for PCA has been listed below. In this code, dataset is in csv format with n columns, where last column is data label and first $n-1$ columns are features for respective data label.

```
# Linear Discriminant Analysis (LDA)
# Importing the libraries
import numpy as np
import matplotlib.pyplot as plt
import pandas as pd

# Importing the dataset
dataset = pd.read_csv('DATASET_NAME.csv')
X = dataset.iloc[:, :n].values
y = dataset.iloc[:, -1].values

# Feature Scaling
from sklearn.preprocessing import StandardScaler
sc = StandardScaler()
X = sc.fit_transform(X)

# Splitting the dataset into the Training set and Test set
from sklearn.model_selection import train_test_split
X_train, X_test, y_train, y_test = train_test_split(X, y, test_size = 0.2,
random_state = 0)

# Applying LDA
from sklearn.discriminant_analysis import LinearDiscriminantAnalysis as LDA
lda = LDA(n_components = 2)
X_train = lda.fit_transform(X_train, y_train)
X_test = lda.transform(X_test)
```

EXERCISES

10.1 What is dimension reduction technique? Discuss the advantages of dimension reduction technique.

10.2 How PCA is different from LDA? Explain.

10.3 Explain different types of dimension reduction techniques.

10.4 Write programs to implement PCA and LDA.

10.5 Write a short note on t-Distributed stochastic neighbor embedding, autoencoders, and isometric mapping.

10.6 Discuss scenarios where dimension reduction can not be applied.

10.7 What are the uses of eigen vectors in PCA?

10.8 How autoencoders are implemented?

10.9 Write a program to implement autoencoders.

10.10 How large dimensions are understood? What are the indications to reduce dimension reduction?

CHAPTER 11

Fuzzy Logic Systems

Fuzzy logic is one of the important technique in soft computing. Fuzzy logic is a form of many-valued logic that deals with reasoning that is approximate rather than precise. It is a mathematical approach to dealing with uncertainty in complex systems, pioneered by Lotfi Zadeh in the 1960s. Traditional (binary) logic is based on true/false, 0/1 values, where statements are either completely true or completely false. Fuzzy logic, on the other hand, allows for partial truths, where something can be true to a certain degree, or false to a certain degree, or even simultaneously true and false to some degree. It's particularly useful in systems where information is incomplete or imprecise, like in artificial intelligence, control systems, decision-making processes, and pattern recognition. Fuzzy logic has been applied in various fields including engineering, robotics, and even in consumer products like washing machines and air conditioners where it helps to provide more flexible and adaptive control systems.

Fuzzy systems typically consist of the following components:

- **Fuzzy Sets:** These are sets characterized by membership functions that assign degrees of membership to elements. Fuzzy sets allow for the representation of uncertainty and vagueness in the system by allowing elements to partially belong to multiple sets simultaneously.
- **Membership Functions:** These functions define the degree of membership of an element in a fuzzy set. They map input data to fuzzy sets by assigning membership values based on how well the input data satisfy the characteristics of each fuzzy set.
- **Fuzzy Logic Operations:** These operations, such as fuzzy AND (union), fuzzy OR (intersection), and fuzzy NOT (complement), are used to manipulate fuzzy sets and apply fuzzy reasoning.
- **Fuzzification:** This stage involves converting crisp input data (data with precise values) into fuzzy sets. Fuzzy sets allow for the representation

of uncertainty or vagueness in the input data. This step is crucial for handling imprecise or incomplete information.

- **Fuzzy Inference System (FIS):** This is the core of a fuzzy system. It involves applying fuzzy logic rules to the fuzzy sets obtained from the fuzzification stage to derive fuzzy output sets. The FIS typically includes following components:
  - ***Fuzzy Rule Base:*** This contains a set of if-then rules that relate input variables to output variables. These rules capture expert knowledge or empirical relationships within the system.
  - ***Fuzzy Inference Engine***: This component interprets the fuzzy rules and performs fuzzy reasoning to determine the appropriate output fuzzy sets based on the input fuzzy sets.
  - ***Defuzzification:*** This step involves converting the fuzzy output sets obtained from the inference process back into crisp output values. Various defuzzification methods, such as centroid or maxima methods, can be used to achieve this.
  - ***Knowledge Base***: This component stores the domain knowledge in the form of linguistic rules or numerical data that govern the behavior of the fuzzy system. It includes the fuzzy rule base and membership functions.

These components work together to enable fuzzy systems to model and reason with uncertain or imprecise information, making them useful for applications where traditional binary logic may not be sufficient. The block diagram of fuzzy logic system has been explained Figure 11.1.

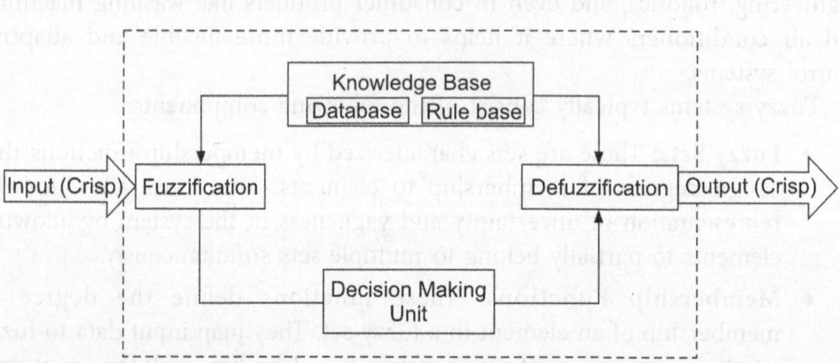

Figure 11.1 Block diagram of fuzzy logic system.

11.1 FUZZY SETS

A fuzzy set is a mathematical concept which is as an extension of classical (crisp) set theory. Unlike classical sets, where an element either belongs or does not belong to a set (binary membership), fuzzy sets allow for degrees of membership, representing the extent to which an element belongs to a set in a graded manner. Formally, a fuzzy set A in a universe of discourse X is characterized by a membership function $\mu_A(x)$, which assigns a degree of membership to each element x in X . The membership function degree $\mu_A(x)$ maps each element x to a value in the interval [0,1], where, $m_A(x) = 0$ indicates that x does not belong to the set A at all, and $m_A(x) = 1$ indicates that x fully belongs to the set A. If value of $m_A(x)$ is between 0 and 1, $0 < \mu_A(x) < 1$ indicates a partial membership of x in A. The membership function can take various forms, such as triangular, trapezoidal, Gaussian or sigmoidal, depending on the nature of the application and the characteristics of the data. Fuzzy sets are the first step in fuzzy logic implementation as it represents input data for next stages.

Fuzzy sets can overlap with each other, meaning that an element can have membership in multiple fuzzy sets simultaneously. This property allows for the representation of complex relationships and intersections between different categories or concepts. The common operations that can be applied to fuzzy sets are union (max), intersection (min), and complement. The example discussed here explain fuzzy sets and its operations. Let A and B be two fuzzy sets such that:

$$A = \left\{ \frac{0.2}{x_1} + \frac{0.4}{x_2} + \frac{0.7}{x_3} + \frac{0.9}{x_4} \right\}, \quad B = \left\{ \frac{0.1}{x_1} + \frac{0.5}{x_2} + \frac{0.4}{x_3} + \frac{0.8}{x_4} \right\}$$

Both sets A and B include four members x_1, x_2, x_3 and x_4. The degree of membership for x_1 in A is 0.2, which can be expressed as $\mu_A(x_1)$. Various operations of A and B are as follows:

Union (max): This operation computes maximum of the values for the member in two sets, $A \cup B = \left\{ \frac{0.2}{x_1} + \frac{0.5}{x_2} + \frac{0.7}{x_3} + \frac{0.9}{x_4} \right\}$.

Intersection (min): This operation computes minimum of the values for the member in two sets, $A \cap B = \left\{ \frac{0.1}{x_1} + \frac{0.4}{x_2} + \frac{0.4}{x_3} + \frac{0.8}{x_4} \right\}$

Complement: This evaluates the complement of a set, where values are complement i.e., $A' = \left\{ \frac{0.8}{x_1} + \frac{0.6}{x_2} + \frac{0.3}{x_3} + \frac{0.1}{x_4} \right\}$

11.2 MEMBERSHIP FUNCTIONS

Fuzzy membership functions define the degree to which elements belong to the set. These functions map elements from the universe of discourse to membership degrees, typically ranging between 0 and 1. There are several types of membership functions commonly used in fuzzy logic. Some of the common membership functions are discussed below:

- **Triangular Membership Function:** This is one of the simplest and most commonly used membership functions. It is characterized by three parameters: the left boundary a, the peak or center b, and the right boundary c. The membership function rises linearly from a to b, reaches its peak at b, and then decreases linearly to c. Mathematically, it can be represented as:

$$\mu(x) = \begin{cases} 0 & \text{if } x \le a \\ \dfrac{x-a}{b-a} & \text{if } a < x < b \\ \dfrac{c-x}{c-b} & \text{if } b \le x < c \\ 0 & \text{if } x \ge c \end{cases}$$

The Figure 11.2 shows the triangular membership function.

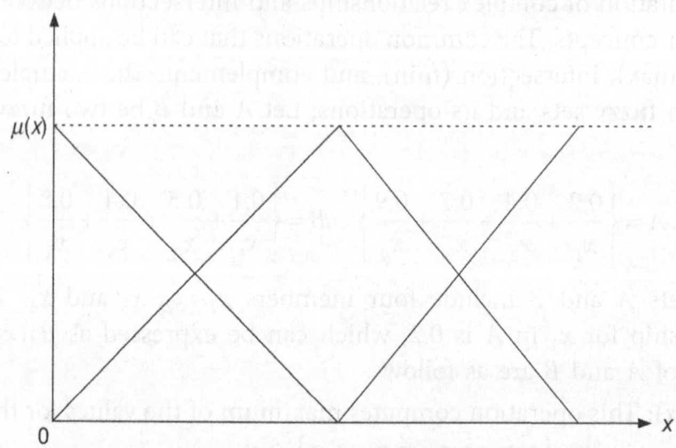

Figure 11.2 Triangular membership function.

- **Trapezoidal Membership Function:** It is similar to the triangular membership function, but with an additional parameter to control the width of the plateau. It is characterized by four parameters: the left boundary a, the left plateau b, the right plateau c, and the right boundary d. The membership function rises linearly from A to b, remains constant at 1 from b to c, and then decreases linearly from c to d. Mathematically, it can be represented as:

$$\mu(x) = \begin{cases} 0 & \text{if } x \le a \\ \dfrac{x-a}{b-a} & \text{if } a < x < b \\ 1 & \text{if } b \le x \le c \\ \dfrac{d-x}{d-c} & \text{if } c < x < d \\ 0 & \text{if } x \ge d \end{cases}$$

The Figure 11.3 shows the trapezoidal membership function.

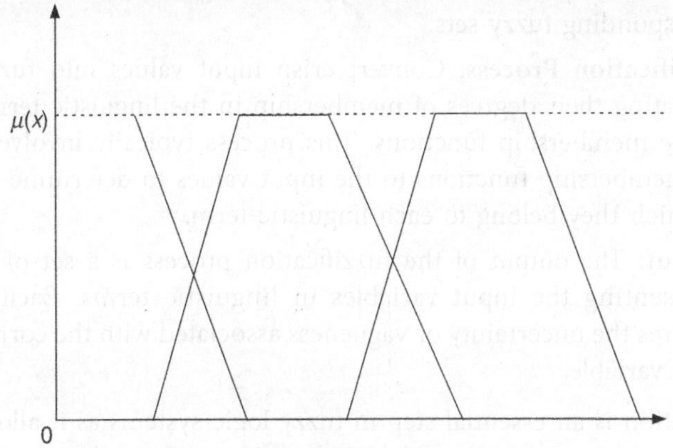

Figure 11.3 Trapezoidal membership function.

- **Gaussian Membership Function:** It is bell-shaped and symmetric around its peak. Characterized by two parameters: the mean μ and the standard deviation σ. It represents the degree of membership as a probability density function following the normal distribution. Mathematically, it can be represented as:

$$\mu(x) = e^{-\frac{(x-\mu)^2}{2\sigma^2}}$$

The choice of membership function depends on the nature of the problem, the shape of the data, and the desired behavior of the fuzzy set.

11.3 FUZZIFICATION

Fuzzification is a process within fuzzy logic where crisp (precise) input data is converted into fuzzy sets. This conversion allows for the representation of uncertainty or vagueness in the input data, enabling fuzzy logic systems to operate on imprecise information. The fuzzification process involves the following steps:

- **Identification of Input Variables:** Identify the crisp input variables relevant to the problem at hand. These variables could be physical quantities, measurements, or other forms of data that need to be processed by the fuzzy logic system.
- **Linguistic Variable Definition:** Define linguistic variables for each input variable. Linguistic variables are terms or labels that describe qualitative aspects of the input variables, such as "low," "medium," and "high."
- **Membership Function Assignment:** Assign membership functions to each linguistic variable. Membership functions describe the degree of

membership of an input value to each linguistic term. These functions define how input values are mapped to degrees of membership in the corresponding fuzzy sets.

- **Fuzzification Process:** Convert crisp input values into fuzzy sets by evaluating their degrees of membership in the linguistic terms defined by the membership functions. This process typically involves applying the membership functions to the input values to determine the degree to which they belong to each linguistic term.
- **Output:** The output of the fuzzification process is a set of fuzzy sets representing the input variables in linguistic terms. Each fuzzy set captures the uncertainty or vagueness associated with the corresponding input variable.

Fuzzification is an essential step in fuzzy logic systems as it allows for the handling of imprecise or incomplete information. Once the input data has been fuzzified, it can be processed using fuzzy inference to make decisions or perform tasks in a fuzzy logic system.

11.4 FUZZY INFERENCE SYSTEM

A fuzzy inference system (FIS) is a computational framework based on fuzzy logic, which aims to model and reason with uncertainty and imprecision in data. It includes rule evaluation as a main step. In this step, fuzzy rules are applied to the fuzzy input values. These rules are typically in the form of "if-then" statements, where the "if" part corresponds to combinations of fuzzy sets of inputs and the "then" part corresponds to fuzzy sets of outputs. Inference engine is next step of FIS. The inference engine evaluates the fuzzy rules to determine the degree to which each rule contributes to the output. It combines the fuzzy sets of inputs according to the fuzzy rules to produce fuzzy sets of outputs. Further, aggregation is another crucial step in FIS. This step involves combining the fuzzy sets of outputs from different rules to obtain a single fuzzy set that represents the overall output. Now, aggregated fuzzy set needs defuzzification as discussed in the next section.

11.5 DEFUZZIFICATION

Defuzzification is the final step after the fuzzy rules have been applied and the outputs have been aggregated into fuzzy sets. Some common methods of defuzzification are discussed below:

- **λ-cut:** A λ cut is a technique used to convert a fuzzy set into a crisp set by defining a threshold value, called the Lambda value (λ), above which membership grades are considered to be fully true (1) and below which membership grades are considered to be fully false (0).

Lambda cuts are commonly employed in fuzzy set theory for various purposes, mainly defuzzification.The first step is to choose a λ value that serves as a threshold for determining the degree of membership in the crisp set. This value determines the level of confidence required for considering a linguistic term to be part of the crisp set. For each linguistic term in the aggregated fuzzy set, its membership grade is compared to the λ value. If the membership grade is greater than or equal to the λ value, the linguistic term is considered to be fully true (1) in the crisp set. Otherwise, it is considered to be fully false (0). Based on the converted membership grades, construct a crisp set that represents the defuzzified output. This crisp set consists of only those linguistic terms whose membership grades meet the threshold set by the λ value. The λ cuts offer flexibility in defuzzification by allowing the adjustment of the threshold for considering linguistic terms as part of the crisp output. Different λ values can lead to different degrees of preciseness or granularity in the defuzzified output.

- **Centroid Method:** This method calculates the center of mass, or centroid, of the aggregated fuzzy set. The crisp output value is then determined based on the centroid position.

  The centroid of the aggregated fuzzy set is calculated as the weighted average of the values in the universe of discourse (the range of possible output values), where each value is weighted by its membership grade in the fuzzy set. The crisp output value is then determined based on the centroid position. This value represents the defuzzified output of the fuzzy inference system. Mathematically, the centroid C of a fuzzy set $A(x)$ with membership function $m_A(x)$ over the universe of discourse X is calculated as:

$$C = \frac{\int_X x \cdot \mu_A(x)\,dx}{\int_X \mu_A(x)\,dx}$$

  where x represents the values in the universe of discourse. $m_A(x)$ is the membership grade of x in the fuzzy set A. The integral is taken over the entire universe of discourse X.

- **Weighted Average Method:** In this approach, each point in the output fuzzy set is weighted by its membership grade, and the crisp output value is calculated as the weighted average of these points. In this method, each value in the universe of discourse (the range of possible output values) is multiplied by its corresponding membership grade in the fuzzy set. These products are then summed up, and the result is divided by the total sum of membership grades. The result of the weighted average calculation represents the crisp output value of the fuzzy inference system. Mathematically, the weighted average $\overline{x}$ of a fuzzy set $A(x)$ with membership function $m_A(x)$ over the universe of discourse X is calculated as:

$$\overline{x} = \frac{\int_X x \cdot \mu_A(x)\,dx}{\int_X \mu_A(x)\,dx}$$

here, the numerator and denominator represent the weighted sum and the total weight, respectively, over the entire universe of discourse X. This method is similar to the centroid method.

- **Mean of Maximum (MOM) Method:** This method selects the maximum value of the aggregated fuzzy set and calculates the crisp output value as the mean of the input values corresponding to this maximum value. The first step is to identify the maximum value of the aggregated fuzzy set. This maximum value corresponds to the degree of membership of the output variable to a certain linguistic value. The crisp output value is determined by taking the mean (average) of the input values corresponding to the maximum value of the aggregated fuzzy set. This involves considering the input values mapped to the linguistic terms that contribute to the maximum membership grade. Mathematically, the Mean of Maximum (MOM) x_{MOM} is calculated as:

$$x_{\text{MOM}} = \frac{\sum_{i=1}^{n} x_i \cdot \mu_i}{\sum_{i=1}^{n} \mu_i}$$

  where, x_i represents the input values corresponding to the linguistic terms contributing to the maximum value of the aggregated fuzzy set. μ_i represents the membership grade of each linguistic term contributing to the maximum value. n is the number of linguistic terms contributing to the maximum value. The MOM method provides a way to obtain a crisp output value that reflects the contributions of the input values corresponding to the most significant linguistic terms in the fuzzy set. It's particularly useful when dealing with multiple linguistic terms contributing to the output simultaneously.

- **Bisector Method:** The bisector method determines the crisp output value as the point, where the area under the left and right portions of the aggregated fuzzy set are equal. It identifies the maximum value of the aggregated fuzzy set. This maximum value corresponds to the degree of membership of the output variable to a certain linguistic value. From the maximum value, two vertical lines are drawn, one to the left and one to the right, bisecting the fuzzy set. These lines divide the fuzzy set into two areas. The crisp output value as the point where the areas under the left and right portions of the fuzzy set are equal is calculated. This point represents the defuzzified output according to the Bisector Method. Mathematically, the Bisector Method finds the crisp output value by finding the point where the cumulative area under the membership function curve on the left side equals the cumulative area on the right side. While the Bisector Method is straightforward conceptually, it may be computationally intensive compared to other defuzzification methods, especially when dealing with complex fuzzy sets or non-symmetric membership functions. However, it provides a balanced approach by considering the distribution of membership grades on both sides of the maximum value.

- **Largest of Maximum (LOM) Method:** This is similar to the MOM method, but instead of taking the mean of the input values corresponding to the maximum value of the aggregated fuzzy set, it simply selects the largest input value corresponding to the maximum value. It identifies the maximum value of the aggregated fuzzy set. This maximum value corresponds to the degree of membership of the output variable to a certain linguistic value. Determine the crisp output value as the largest input value corresponding to the maximum value of the aggregated fuzzy set. In other words, find the linguistic term with the highest membership grade and return the input value associated with that term. Mathematically, the LOM method selects the largest input value corresponding to the maximum value of the aggregated fuzzy set. The LOM method provides a simple and straightforward way to obtain a crisp output value from a fuzzy set. It prioritizes the most significant linguistic term by selecting the largest input value associated with the maximum membership grade. This method is particularly useful when there is a clear preference for certain linguistic terms in the fuzzy output.

The choice of defuzzification method depends on the specific application and requirements. Each method has its advantages and disadvantages in terms of complexity, computational efficiency and accuracy.

11.6 FUZZY LOGIC EXAMPLE

This section demonstrates the working of fuzzy logic with an example. The following should be implemented in a sequential order.

Identify Input and Output variables; decide the descriptor for the task; define membership functions for the input and output variables; form the rule base; rule evaluation and defuzzification.

Let us assume that the problem is related to dirt and grease of washing machine, and its parameters are given in percentage. The output is the respective wash time for the given input. The descriptors for the input are Dirt and Grease. The Dirt could be Small Dirt (SD), Medium Dirt (MD) and Large Dirt (LD). Similarly, Grease could be No Grease (NG), Medium Grease (MG) and Large

Grease (LG). The output variable wash time could be Very Short (VS), Short (S), Medium (M), Large (L) and Very Large (VL). We have used triangular membership function in this example. The dirt membership function range is listed below. For short dirt, $\mu_{SD}(x)$, range is upto 50. Similarly, for $\mu_{MD}(x)$ and $\mu_{LD}(x)$, respective ranges are selected as shown in Figure 11.4.

$$\mu_{SD}(x) = \frac{50 - x}{50} \text{ if } 0 \leq x \leq 50$$

$$\mu_{MD}(x) = \begin{cases} \dfrac{x}{50} & \text{if } 0 \leq x \leq 50 \\ \dfrac{100 - x}{50} & \text{if } 50 \leq x \leq 100 \end{cases}$$

$$\mu_{LD}(x) = \frac{x - 50}{50} \text{ if } 50 \leq x \leq 100$$

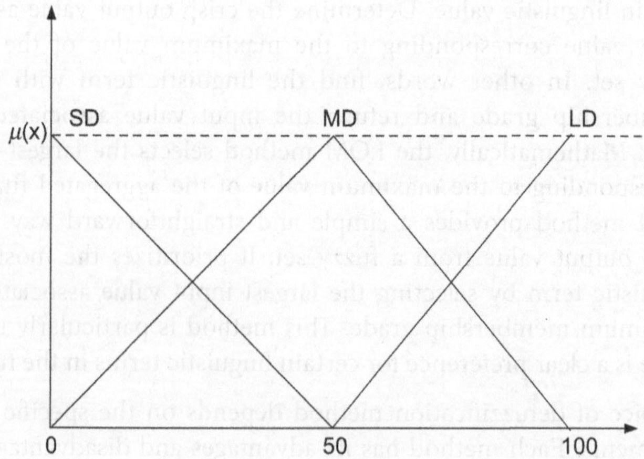

Figure 11.4 Triangular membership function for Dirt.

Similarly, grease membership range is listed below and its ranges are shown in Figure 11.5.

$$\mu_{NG}(y) = \frac{50 - y}{50} \text{ if } 0 \leq y \leq 50$$

$$\mu_{MG}(y) = \begin{cases} \dfrac{y}{50} & \text{if } 0 \leq y \leq 50 \\ \dfrac{100 - y}{50} & \text{if } 50 \leq y \leq 100 \end{cases}$$

$$\mu_{LG}(y) = \frac{y - 50}{50} \text{ if } 50 \leq y \leq 100$$

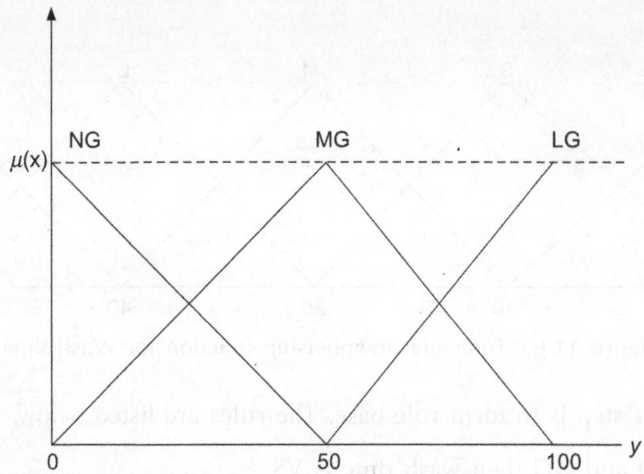

Figure 11.5 Triangular membership function for Grease.

For the output variable wash time, membership function ranges are as follows:

$$\mu_{VS}(z) = \frac{10-z}{10} \text{ if } 0 \le y \le 10$$

$$\mu_S(z) = \begin{cases} \dfrac{z}{10} & \text{if } 0 \le y \le 10 \\ \dfrac{25-z}{15} & \text{if } 10 \le y \le 25 \end{cases}$$

$$\mu_M(z) = \begin{cases} \dfrac{z-10}{15} & \text{if } 10 \le y \le 25 \\ \dfrac{40-z}{15} & \text{if } 25 \le y \le 40 \end{cases}$$

$$\mu_L(z) = \begin{cases} \dfrac{z-25}{15} & \text{if } 25 \le y \le 40 \\ \dfrac{60-z}{20} & \text{if } 40 \le y \le 60 \end{cases}$$

$$\mu_{VL}(z) = \frac{z-40}{20} \text{ if } 40 \le y \le 60$$

The membership function for wash time has been shown in Figure 11.6.

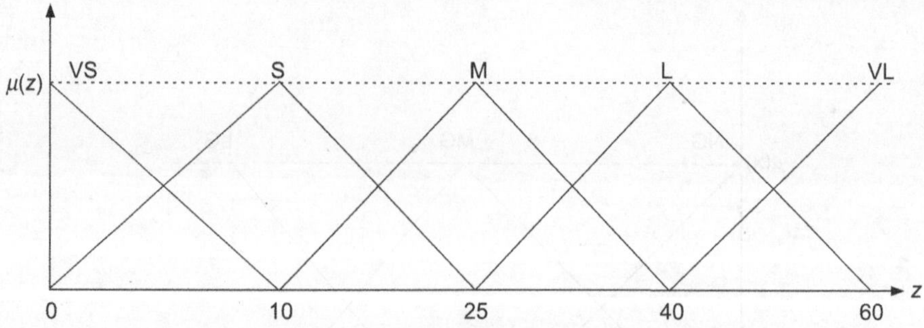

Figure 11.6 Triangular membership function for Wash time.

The next step is to form rule base. The rules are listed below.

- if SD and NG then wash time is VS.
- if SD and MG then wash time is M.
- if SD and LG then wash time is L.
- if MD and NG then wash time is S.
- if MD and MG then wash time is M.
- if MD and LG then wash time is L.
- if LD and NG then wash time is M.
- if LD and MG then wash time is L.
- if LD and LG then wash time is VL.

The above rules are presented in grid view as shown in Figure 11.7.

x \ y	NG	MG	LG
SD	VS	M	L
MD	S	M	L
LD	M	L	VL

Figure 11.7 Grid view of the rules.

Now, assume that the dirt level is 60% and grease level is 70%. Only four membership functions are applicable for dirt (60) and grease (70). These are $\mu_{MD}(x)$, $\mu_{LD}(x)$, $\mu_{MG}(x)$ and $\mu_{LG}(x)$. We put the values of dirt and grease in membership functions as follows:

$$\mu_{MD}(x) = \frac{100 - x}{50} \quad \text{if } 50 \le x \le 100$$

as x = 60, $\mu_{\text{MD}}(60) = \frac{4}{5}$. Similarly, $\mu_{\text{LD}}(60) = \frac{1}{5}$.

For, $\mu_{MG}(y) = \frac{100-y}{50}$ if $50 \le y \le 100$,

as y = 70, $\mu_{\text{MG}}(70) = \frac{3}{5}$. Similarly, $\mu_{\text{LG}}(70) = \frac{2}{5}$.

As all rules include 'AND', the operator 'min' will be applicable and 'max' of 'min' is the output (max-min and max-product are two common operations).

$$S_1 = \min(\mu_{MD}(60), \mu_{MG}(70)) = \min\left(\frac{4}{5}, \frac{3}{5}\right) = \frac{3}{5}$$

$$S_2 = \min(\mu_{MD}(60), \mu_{LG}(70)) = \min\left(\frac{4}{5}, \frac{2}{5}\right) = \frac{2}{5}$$

$$S_3 = \min(\mu_{LD}(60), \mu_{MG}(70)) = \min\left(\frac{1}{5}, \frac{3}{5}\right) = \frac{1}{5}$$

$$S_4 = \min(\mu_{LD}(60), \mu_{LG}(70)) = \min\left(\frac{1}{5}, \frac{2}{5}\right) = \frac{1}{5}$$

therefore, $\max(S_1, S_2, S_3, S_4) = \max\left(\frac{3}{5}, \frac{2}{5}, \frac{1}{5}, \frac{1}{5}\right) = \frac{3}{5}$

The value $\frac{3}{5}$ is for the rule $\mu_{\text{MD}}(60)$, $\mu_{\text{MG}}(70)$, it has been shown in Figure 11.8.

x \ y	NG	MG	LG
SD	X	X	X
MD	X	M	L
LD	X	L	VL

x \ y	NG	MG	LG
SD	X	X	X
MD	X	3/5	2/5
LD	X	1/5	1/5

Figure 11.8 Grid view of the rules for the output.

Finally, we put the value for membership function of $\mu_{\text{MD}}(60)$ and $\mu_{\text{MG}}(70)$ as follows:

$$\mu_M(z) = \frac{z-10}{15} \text{ if } 10 \le y \le 25$$

$$\mu_M(z) = \frac{3}{5}, \frac{3}{5} = \frac{z-10}{15}$$

$\Rightarrow z$ = 19. Similarly,

$$\mu_M(z) = \frac{40-z}{25} \text{ if } 25 \le y \le 40$$

$$\frac{3}{5} = \frac{40 - z}{25}$$

$\Rightarrow z = 31$. Now, we compute the mean value for respective z values as:

$$\text{Wash time} = \text{mean}(19, 31) = 25$$

Therefore, wash time is computed as 25 min.

EXERCISES

11.1 Discuss fuzzy logic as a soft computing technique.

11.2 Differentiate between crisp and fuzzy values.

11.3 How fuzzy values are different from probability? Explain.

11.4 Write a note on fuzzy sets.

11.5 Discuss fuzzy membership functions.

11.6 What is fuzzification? Explain.

11.7 Discuss fuzzy inference system in detail.

11.8 Discuss working of defuzzification.

11.9 Write note on different defuzzification techniques.

11.10 Discuss an example to calculate tip of food in restaurant based on food quality, service quality and restaurant ambience.

11.11 Write programs to implement the above fuzzy example and the example solved in this chapter.

11.12 Discuss max-min and max-product with examples.

11.13 Discuss fuzzy operations using examples.

CHAPTER 12

Genetic Algorithms

A Genetic Algorithm (GA) is a type of optimization algorithm inspired by the principles of natural selection and genetics. It is commonly used to find optimal or near-optimal solutions to optimization and search problems. The concept of genetic algorithms was introduced by John Holland in the 1960s. Holland, an American scientist, was a pioneer in the fields of complex adaptive systems and evolutionary computation. He developed genetic algorithms as a computational model for simulating the process of natural selection and evolution. Holland's work on genetic algorithms laid the foundation for the field of evolutionary computation, which encompasses a range of optimization and search algorithms inspired by biological evolution. His seminal book "Adaptation in Natural and Artificial Systems," published in 1975, provided a comprehensive overview of genetic algorithms and their applications. Since then, GA have become one of the most widely used techniques in optimization, machine learning and artificial intelligence. The GA mainly includes initialization of population, evaluation, selection, crossover, mutation, replacement and termination as common steps. Genetic algorithms are versatile and can be applied to a wide range of optimization problems, from engineering and finance to artificial intelligence and beyond. They offer advantages, such as parallelism, robustness and the ability to handle complex search spaces. However, they may require careful tuning of parameters and can be computationally expensive for certain problems. The sequential flow of GA steps has been explained in Algorithm 12.

Algorithm 12 Pseudocode for genetic algorithm working

1. **Initialization:** Generate an initial population of individuals randomly or using some heuristic method.
2. **Evaluation:** Evaluate the fitness of each individual in the population using a fitness function.
3. **Termination Criteria Check:** Check if termination criteria are met (e.g., maximum number of generations reached, satisfactory fitness level achieved). If criteria met, exit.

4. **Selection:** Select individuals from the current population to create a mating pool based on their fitness. Common selection methods include roulette wheel selection, tournament selection and rank-based selection.
5. **Crossover:** Perform crossover on pairs of individuals from the mating pool to create offspring. Common crossover techniques include single-point crossover, multi-point crossover and uniform crossover.
6. **Mutation:** Introduce random changes (mutation) to the genetic material of offspring with a low probability.
7. **Replacement:** Replace the current population with the new offspring population. Optionally, apply elitism to ensure the best individuals from the current generation are carried over to the next.
8. Go to Step 2 (Evaluation).

12.1 INITIALIZATION

In genetic algorithms, initialization refers to the process of creating the initial population of potential solutions or individuals. This population is generated randomly or using some heuristic method to ensure diversity and coverage of the solution space. The common components of initialization process are discussed below:

- **Population Size Determination:** Determine the size of the population, i.e., the number of individuals in each generation. This is usually decided based on the complexity of the problem and computational constraints.
- **Chromosome Representation:** Decide how to represent individuals in the population. This could be binary strings, integer arrays, real-valued vectors, or any other suitable representation for the problem domain.
- **Random Initialization:** Generate the initial population randomly. This involves creating a set of individuals, each with a random set of genes within the defined problem constraints. The randomness helps in maintaining diversity within the population.
- **Heuristic Initialization:** In some cases, instead of random initialization, a heuristic approach might be used to create the initial population. This could involve using domain-specific knowledge to generate better-quality initial solutions.

The purpose of initialization is to start with a diverse set of potential solutions that cover the solution space adequately. This diversity ensures that the genetic algorithm can explore a wide range of solutions and hopefully converge towards a good solution efficiently through the evolutionary process of selection, crossover and mutation.

12.2 EVALUATION

In genetic algorithms, evaluation is the process of assessing the fitness or quality of each individual in the population. The evaluation step is crucial as it determines which individuals are more likely to survive and reproduce in subsequent generations. First define a fitness function that quantitatively measures how well an individual solves the problem at hand. The fitness function evaluates the performance of an individual solution against the optimization criteria of the problem. This function is often problem-specific and reflects the objectives of the optimization problem. Next step, for each individual in the population, apply the fitness function to compute its fitness score. This involves analyzing the individual's solution representation and determining its fitness value based on the problem's requirements. The fitness value could be a single scalar value or a multi-dimensional vector depending on the problem's nature. Once the fitness scores are calculated for all individuals, they are typically ranked or scaled based on their fitness values. This step helps in identifying the relative performance of individuals within the population. Common techniques include ranking individuals based on their fitness scores or performing fitness scaling to adjust the fitness values to a desired range. The evaluation process plays a crucial role in the selection process, where individuals with higher fitness scores are more likely to be selected for reproduction (e.g., through methods like roulette wheel selection, tournament selection, or rank-based selection). By favoring individuals with better fitness, the algorithm directs its search towards promising regions of the solution space. Evaluation also helps in determining when to terminate the evolutionary process. The termination criterion could be reaching a maximum number of generations, achieving a satisfactory fitness threshold or other stopping conditions specified by the user.

12.3 SELECTION

Selection is a key component of genetic algorithms that determines which individuals from the current population will be chosen to produce offspring for the next generation. The goal of selection is to favor individuals with higher fitness, increasing the likelihood that their genetic material will be passed on to subsequent generations, mimicking the principle of "survival of the fittest" from natural selection. Common selection methods used in genetic algorithms are discussed below:

- **Roulette Wheel Selection:** In this method, individuals are selected with a probability proportional to their fitness scores. Individuals with higher fitness have a greater chance of being selected, however, all individuals have a non-zero chance. It is like spinning a roulette wheel where each individual's fitness score determines the size of their slice of the wheel.
- **Tournament Selection:** In tournament selection, a small subset of individuals is randomly selected from the population and the individual

with the highest fitness within that subset is chosen as a parent. This process is repeated until a sufficient number of parents are selected for reproduction. The tournament size (number of individuals in each tournament) is a parameter that can be adjusted based on the problem.

- **Rank-based Selection:** This method ranks individuals in the population based on their fitness scores, rather than considering the actual fitness values. Individuals are then selected based on their rank rather than their fitness scores. This approach ensures that selection pressure remains consistent across generations, regardless of the absolute fitness values.
- **Stochastic Universal Sampling:** Stochastic universal sampling is a variation of roulette wheel selection where multiple "pointers" are placed on the roulette wheel, spaced evenly. The wheel is then spun once and individuals are selected based on the pointers' positions. This method ensures a more even distribution of selected individuals and reduces the likelihood of prematurely converging to suboptimal solutions.
- **Elitism:** Elitism involves preserving a certain number of the best individuals from the current generation and directly transferring them to the next generation without any changes. This ensures that the best solutions found so far are not lost during the evolutionary process.

By favoring individuals with higher fitness, selection enables genetic algorithms to iteratively improve the quality of solutions over successive generations.

12.4 CROSSOVER

Crossover, also known as recombination, is a genetic operator in genetic algorithms that mimics the mating process in natural genetics. It involves combining genetic information from two parent individuals to create offspring with potentially better traits or solutions. Crossover is a key step in GAs for exploring new areas of the solution space and promoting diversity among the population. In crossover, a crossover point or multiple crossover points are randomly selected along the chromosomes of the parent individuals. These crossover points determine where the genetic material will be exchanged between the parents to create offspring. Once the crossover points are determined, the genetic material between the parents' chromosomes is exchanged to create offspring chromosomes. This exchange can occur in various ways depending on the crossover method used. Common crossover methods are single point, multiple points, uniform and arithmetic crossover. In single point, a single crossover point is selected and genetic material from one parent is swapped with genetic material from the other parent at that point. In case of multiple crossover points, multiple points are selected and segments of genetic material are swapped between parents at these points. In uniform crossover, each gene in the offspring is randomly selected from one of the parents with equal probability. In arithmetic crossover, for real-valued representations, offspring genes are computed as a weighted average of the corresponding genes of the parents. Crossover promotes the exploration of the solution space by combining beneficial traits from different parents, thereby increasing the diversity of the population and potentially leading to improved solutions over time. However, the effectiveness of crossover depends on factors, such as the representation of individuals, the problem's characteristics and the choice of crossover parameters.

12.5 MUTATION

Mutation is another genetic operator in genetic algorithms serving as a mechanism to introduce random changes in individuals' genetic material. Unlike crossover, which involves recombination of genetic information from parents, mutation alters individual chromosomes directly, typically by randomly modifying gene values. Mutation plays a crucial role in maintaining genetic diversity within the population and preventing premature convergence to suboptimal solutions. Mutation rate is important in implementing this step. A mutation rate parameter indicates the probability of a gene in an individual undergoing mutation. This rate is typically a small value, ensuring that mutation occurs infrequently but still allowing for exploration of new regions of the solution space. For each individual in the population, genes are randomly selected for mutation based on the mutation rate. A random number generator is commonly used to determine whether each gene undergoes mutation, with the probability of mutation determined by the mutation rate. If a gene is selected for mutation, its value is randomly perturbed or altered in some way. The specific mutation operation depends on the representation of the individuals and the problem domain. Common mutation operations include bit flip, Gaussian and swap mutation. Bit flip mutation is used for binary representations, where a randomly selected bit is flipped from 0 to 1 or vice versa. Gaussian mutation is used for real-valued representations, where a small random value drawn from a Gaussian distribution is added to the gene's current value. Swap mutation is used for permutation-based representations, where two genes within the chromosome are randomly swapped. The mutated individuals are introduced into the population, typically through replacement of existing individuals. This ensures that the population maintains diversity and allows potentially beneficial mutations to propagate through the generations. Mutation serves as a mechanism for introducing novel genetic material into the population, allowing the genetic algorithm to explore new regions of the solution space and potentially discover better solutions. By introducing random changes, mutation complements the selective pressure exerted by crossover and helps prevent premature convergence to local optima. The mutation rate and mutation operation are important parameters that can significantly influence the performance of the genetic algorithm.

12.6 REPLACEMENT

Replacement is the process of determining which individuals from the current population will be replaced by new individuals, typically offspring generated through crossover and mutation, to form the next generation. Replacement strategies are crucial for maintaining diversity within the population and guiding the evolutionary process towards better solutions. Common procedure for replacement are generational, elitist, steady-state, tournament, and fitness-based replacement. In generational replacement, the entire population of the current generation is replaced by the offspring generated from the parents. All individuals in the current population are discarded, and only the offspring become the new population. This approach ensures a complete refresh of the population, potentially allowing for more drastic changes in the search space. Elitism involves preserving a certain number of the best individuals (elite individuals) from the current population and directly transferring them to the next generation without any changes. The remaining slots in the population are filled with offspring generated through crossover and mutation. Elitism helps to ensure that the best solutions found so far are not lost during the evolutionary process and can serve as a baseline for comparison in subsequent generations. In steady-state replacement, only a subset of individuals in the current population is replaced by offspring, while the rest of the population remains unchanged. Offspring replace the least fit individuals in the population, maintaining a constant population size. This approach allows for a more gradual evolution of the population and can help preserve diversity. Tournament replacement involves selecting pairs of individuals (parents and offspring) and comparing their fitness values. The least fit individual in each pair is replaced by the corresponding offspring, ensuring that only the fittest individuals survive to the next generation. This method allows for competition between parents and offspring, favoring the selection of the best individuals for the next generation. Fitness-based replacement involves ranking individuals in the combined parent-offspring population based on their fitness values. A certain percentage of the least fit individuals are replaced by offspring, with the remaining individuals selected from the parents or offspring based on their fitness values. This approach aims to strike a balance between preserving diversity and favoring individuals with higher fitness values. The choice of replacement strategy depends on various factors such as the problem domain, population size, computational resources, and the desired balance between exploration and exploitation. Each replacement strategy has its advantages and trade-offs in terms of maintaining diversity, preserving good solutions, and guiding the search towards optimal or near-optimal solutions.

12.7 GENETIC ALGORITHM EXAMPLE

This section explains a simple example of solving a maximization problem step by step using a genetic algorithm. In this example, we will solve the problem of finding the maximum value of a mathematical function $f(x) = x_2$, where x is an integer number in the range [0, 32]. (we understand that the answer is easy, however, simple problems are easy to explain and could easily infer complicated steps involved in complex or computationally large problems).

1. **Initialization:** Decide on the size of the population. Let's say we choose a population size of 10 individuals. For chromosome representation, represent each individual as a real number x within the range [0, 32]. Random initialization generates the initial population with random values for x within the specified range.
2. **Evaluation:** Fitness function is used to evaluate the fitness of each individual. In this case, the fitness is the value of the function $f(x) = x^2$. Evaluate the fitness of each individual by calculating $f(x) = x^2$ for each x value in the population.
3. **Selection:** Choose a selection method, such as roulette wheel selection, tournament selection or rank-based selection. Select individuals from the population for reproduction based on their fitness values. Higher fitness individuals are more likely to be selected.
4. **Crossover:** Define a crossover rate (probability) for crossover to occur between selected individuals. Apply crossover to pairs of selected individuals to produce offspring. Let's use single-point crossover as the crossover operation.
5. **Mutation:** Define a mutation rate (probability) for mutation to occur in offspring. Apply mutation to the offspring population. Let's use a small random perturbation to mutate the gene values.
6. **Replacement:** Choose a replacement strategy, such as generational replacement, elitist replacement or steady-state replacement. Replace individuals in the current population with the offspring population based on the chosen replacement strategy.
7. **Termination:** Decide on a termination criterion, such as reaching a maximum number of generations or achieving a satisfactory fitness threshold. Check if the termination criterion is met. If not, repeat steps 2 to 6 until the termination criterion is satisfied.
8. **Solution Extraction:** Extract the best individual from the final population, which represents the solution to the optimization problem. Obtain the output value x corresponding to the best individual as the solution to the maximization problem.

The code in Python explaining the working of this example $f(x) = x^2$ is as follows:

```
import random, math
def generate_population(size, x_boundaries):
    lower_x_boundary, upper_x_boundary = x_boundaries
    population = []
    for i in range(size):
```

```
        individual = {
        "x": random.uniform(lower_x_boundary, upper_x_boundary),
        }
        population.append(individual)
    return population

def apply_function(individual):
    x = individual["x"]
    return x**2

def choice_by_roulette(sorted_population, fitness_sum):
    offset = 0
    normalized_fitness_sum = fitness_sum
    lowest_fitness = apply_function(sorted_population[0])
    if lowest_fitness < 0:
        offset = -lowest_fitness
        normalized_fitness_sum += offset * len(sorted_population)
    draw = random.uniform(0, 1)
    accumulated = 0
    for individual in sorted_population:
        fitness = apply_function(individual) + offset
        probability = fitness / normalized_fitness_sum
        accumulated += probability
        if draw <= accumulated:
            return individual

def sort_population_by_fitness(population):
    return sorted(population, key=apply_function)

def crossover(individual_a, individual_b):
    xa = individual_a["x"]
    xb = individual_b["x"]
    return {"x": (xa + xb) / 2}

def mutate(individual):
    next_x = individual["x"] + random.uniform(0, 5)
    lower_boundary, upper_boundary = (0, 32)
    # Guarantee we keep inside boundaries
    next_x = min(max(next_x, lower_boundary), upper_boundary)
    return {"x": next_x}

def make_next_generation(previous_population):
    next_generation = []
    sorted_by_fitness_population =
```

```
    sort_population_by_fitness(previous_population)
    population_size = len(previous_population)
    fitness_sum = sum(apply_function(individual) for
    individual in population)
    for i in range(population_size):
        first_choice = choice_by_roulette(sorted_by_fitness_population,
        fitness_sum)
        second_choice = choice_by_roulette(sorted_by_fitness_population,
        fitness_sum)
        individual = crossover(first_choice, second_choice)
        individual = mutate(individual)
        next_generation.append(individual)
    return next_generation

#Script now...
generations = 10
population = generate_population(size=10, x_boundaries=(0,32))
i = 1
while True:
    print(f" GENERATION {i}")
    for individual in population:
        print(individual, apply_function(individual))
    if i == generations:
        break
    i += 1
    population = make_next_generation(population)

best_individual = sort_population_by_fitness(population)[-1]
print("\n FINAL RESULT")
print(best_individual, apply_function(best_individual))
```

EXERCISES

12.1 What is evolutionary algorithm? Discuss genetic algorithm as a type of evolutionary algorithm.

12.2 Discuss the workflow of a genetic algorithm.

12.3 How population initialized performed in genetic algorithm? Discuss various population initialization techniques.

12.4 Write a short note on selection techniques. How will you select suitable selection technique?

12.5 Discuss various crossover methods.

12.6 Discuss various mutation methods.

12.7 What is mutation rate? Explain with an example.

12.8 How is replacement performed in genetic algorithm? Is it required one time or multiple times in an iteration?

12.9 Discuss termination criteria in genetic algorithm.

12.10 What is optimal solution? Explain in context of genetic algorithm.

12.11 Write a program to implement genetic algorithm to find optimal value of a cubic function.

12.12 Write a program to implement genetic algorithm to find best path in a graph for fixed source and target nodes.

12.13 Which fitness function you will select and why?

12.14 Can we find travelling salesman problem solution using genetic algorithm? Justify.

12.15 Does genetic algorithm converge? Explain.

Bibliography

[1] Charu C. Aggarwal. *Neural Networks and Deep Learning: A Textbook.* Springer, 2018.

[2] Valentina Emilia Balas, Lakhmi C Jain, Marius Mircea Balas, and Dumitru Baleanu. *Soft Computing Applications: Proceedings of the 9th International Workshop Soft Computing Applications (SOFA 2020)*, Volume 1438. Springer Nature, 2023.

[3] Siddhartha Bhattacharyya, Paramartha Dutta, and Susanta Chakraborty. *Hybrid Soft Computing Approaches: Research and Applications*, Volume 611. Springer, 2015.

[4] Christopher M. Bishop. *Pattern Recognition and Machine Learning.* Springer, 2006.

[5] Margaret A. Boden. *Artificial Intelligence: A Very Short Introduction.* Oxford University Press, 2018.

[6] Thomas Bäck, David B Fogel, and Zbigniew Michalewicz. *Evolutionary Computation 1: Basic Algorithms and Operators.* CRC Press, 1997.

[7] Carlos A Coello Coello, Gary B Lamont, and David A Van Veldhuizen. *Evolutionary Algorithms for Solving Multi-Objective Problems.* Springer, 2007.

[8] Jack Copeland. *Artificial Intelligence: A Philosophical Introduction.* Blackwell Publishers, 1993.

[9] Nello Cristianini and John Shawe-Taylor. *An Introduction to Support Vector Machines and Other Kernel-based Learning Methods.* Cambridge University Press, 2000.

[10] Richard O. Duda, Peter E. Hart, and David G. Stork. *Pattern Classification.* Wiley, 2012.

[11] Rich Elaine, Knight Kevin, and Nair Shivashankar, B. *Artificial Intelligence.* McGraw-Hill, 3rd edition, 2013.

[12] Brian S Everitt, Sabine Landau, and Morven Leese. *Cluster Analysis*. John Wiley & Sons, 2011.

[13] António Gaspar-Cunha, Ricardo Takahashi, and Ricardo Jardim-Gonçalves, editors. *Soft Computing Applications in Industry*. Springer, 2010.

[14] Pierre Geurts, Damien Ernst, and Louis Wehenkel. *Random Forests for Classification*. Springer, 2006.

[15] David E Goldberg. *Genetic Algorithms in Search, Optimization, and Machine Learning*. Addison-Wesley, 1989.

[16] Ian Goodfellow, Yoshua Bengio, and Aaron Courville. *Deep Learning*. MIT Press, 2016.

[17] Aurélien Géron. *Hands-On Machine Learning with Scikit-Learn, Keras, and Tensor Flow*. O'Reilly Media, 2019.

[18] Jiawei Han, Micheline Kamber, and Jian Pei. *Data Mining: Concepts and Techniques*. Elsevier, 2011.

[19] Robin Hanson. *The Age of Em: Work, Love, and Life when Robots Rule the Earth*. Oxford University Press, 2016.

[20] Jeff Heaton. *Artificial Intelligence for Humans*. CreateSpace Independent Publishing Platform, 2014.

[21] S.K. Jain, Lakhmi C. Jain, and J.C. Bansal. *Soft Computing: Techniques and its Applications in Electrical Engineering*. Springer, 2008.

[22] Gareth James, Daniela Witten, Trevor Hastie, and Robert Tibshirani. *An Introduction to Statistical Learning: with Applications in R*. Springer, 2013.

[23] George J Klir and Bo Yuan. *Fuzzy Sets and Fuzzy Logic: Theory and Applications*. Prentice-Hall PTR, 1995.

[24] Daphne Koller and Nir Friedman. *Probabilistic Graphical Models: Principles and Techniques*. MIT Press, 2009.

[25] Max Kuhn and Kjell Johnson. *Applied Predictive Modeling*. Springer, 2013.

[26] Boris Mirkin. *Clustering for Data Mining: A Data Recovery Approach*. CRC Press, 2005.

[27] Javier Montero, Mario Pérez, and Francisco Herrera. *Soft Computing for Complex Multiple Criteria Decision Making*. Springer, 2006.

[28] Kevin P. Murphy. *Machine Learning: A Probabilistic Perspective*. MIT Press, 2012.

[29] Andreas C. Müller and Sarah Guido. *Introduction to Machine Learning with Python: A Guide for Data Scientists*. O'Reilly Media, 2016.

[30] Nils J. Nilsson. *Artificial Intelligence: A New Synthesis*. Elsevier, 1998.

[31] Nils J. Nilsson. *The Quest for Artificial Intelligence*. Cambridge University Press, 2009.

[32] Daniel L. Osherson, Michael Stob, Scott Weinstein, and Ofer H. Tchernichovski. *Unsupervised Learning: Foundations of Neural Computation*. MIT Press, 1996.

[33] David L. Poole and Alan K. Mackworth. *Artificial Intelligence: Foundations of Computational Agents*. Cambridge University Press, 2017.

[34] Timothy J Ross. *Fuzzy Logic with Engineering Applications*. McGraw-Hill, 1995.

[35] Stuart Russell and Peter Norvig. *Artificial Intelligence: A Modern Approach*. Pearson, 2016.

[36] Bernhard Sch¨olkopf and Alexander J Smola. *Learning with Kernels: Support Vector Machines, Regularization, Optimization, and Beyond*. MIT Press, 2001.

[37] Shai Shalev-Shwartz and Shai Ben-David. *Understanding Machine Learning: From Theory to Algorithms*. Cambridge University Press, 2014.

[38] Shishir K Shandilya, Smita Shandilya, Kusum Deep and Atulya K Nagar. *Handbook of Research on Soft Computing and Nature-inspired Algorithms*. IGI Global, 2017.

[39] SN Sivanandam and SN Deepa. *Principles of Soft Computing (with CD)*. John Wiley & Sons, 2007.

[40] Pang-Ning Tan, Michael Steinbach, and Vipin Kumar. *Introduction to Data Mining*. Pearson, 2005.

[41] Kevin Warwick. *Artificial Intelligence: The Basics*. Routledge, 2012.

[42] Xin Yao. *Introduction to Evolutionary Algorithms*. Springer, 1999.

[43] John Yen and Reza Langari. *Fuzzy Logic: Intelligence, Control, and Information*. Prentice-Hall PTR, 1999.

Index